Home Improvements
a DIY guide
David Johnson

published in association with Marley Ltd.

STANLEY PAUL, LONDON

Home Improvements
a DIY guide

STANLEY PAUL & CO LTD
3 Fitzroy Square, London W1

An imprint of the Hutchinson Group

London Melbourne Sydney Auckland Wellington
Johannesburg Cape Town and agencies throughout the world

First published 1973

This book has been set in Journal type by Whitefriars Press,
printed by offset litho at Ebenezer Baylis of Leicester
and bound by William Brendon at Tiptree

Produced by Hutchinson Benham Limited
Designed by Design Practitioners Limited

ISBN 0 09 117121 0

Contents

Since March 1957, when I produced the first issue of the successful monthly magazine *Do it yourself*, I have been at the very centre of a great self-help movement which has affected the lives of many millions of people in this country.

I have seen countless examples of first-class work in the improvement and maintenance of homes by unskilled men and women; I have marvelled at some of the fantastic results achieved at conversion of derelict property and the achievements of many amateurs in building their own superior houses and bungalows.

I believe that every man and woman has an innate skill only awaiting a little encouragement and advice for it to be brought into action to provide a use of leisure which can be both pleasurable and profitable.

The aim of this book is to show how, in simple language and clear instruction, homeowners and many tenants of rented accommodation can repair, improve and maintain their property and its surroundings by the use of readily available products and services at the lowest possible cost.

I am grateful to Marley Ltd. of Sevenoaks for giving me this opportunity to present to you a simple DIY guide to home improvements with the hope that you, too, will find full expression to your talents for making your home not only enhanced in value but a bright, labour-saving, happy place which you have created by your own efforts.

D.J.

(1) The case for do-it-yourself

During the past few years an astonishing, and quite unparalleled, change has taken place in this country affecting the lives of almost every person looking for living accommodation.

They have become increasingly aware that the new home for which they have scraped and saved gets more out of reach as the months pass.

They have noted statements in the Press that the price of new houses mortgaged with building societies rose by over £2,400—from £5,462 to £7,899—between the first quarter of 1971 and the third quarter of 1972 and there appears to be no end to the escalation.

But even these prices apply only to very moderate standards of housing for they have only to look at any selection of House for Sale announcements to realise that the day of the £12,000-£15,000, three-bedroomed semi-detached property is already here.

Fortunate indeed is the house-owner free of mortgage who can look at his property and say, 'This is my castle which I will protect against all-comers'.

But it is not only house purchase which is the major problem for engaged couples. The question of improving a property whose price has stretched their purse to the limit is now an alarming one, for costs of professional labour are at an all-time high—even when householders are lucky enough to find a local firm to do the work at anything like a price they can afford.

It is certainly true that most people today look upon their property as the finest possible investment and realise that every effort must be made to keep it in first class order. They know only too well that while domestic purchases decrease in value over the years there is real investment value arising from home improvements in the form of additions to the home; be it a garage, a sun lounge or a patio.

It is equally true that there are very few people, apart from the infirm and the elderly, who cannot spare a little of their increasing leisure time for jobs in and around the house.

Let me put the case for do-it-yourself quite simply:

1 Initially it can save you a lot of money.

2 Money used for do-it-yourself is not money *spent*, it is an investment which will pay rich dividends in the future.

3 It is a pastime, unlike many others, which produces a worthwhile end product.

4 The physical activity involved in many DIY programmes is conducive to good health. DIY has a real therapeutic value.

5 Self-confidence arising from successful accomplishment of tasks considered outside your scope is a worthwhile asset in these highly competitive days. You can never tell when additional abilities gained from your DIY activity may not win better rewards.

How you will set about your DIY home improvement plan and join the ten million others who make profitable and pleasurable use of their leisure is detailed in subsequent chapters.

But before you begin on a home improvement plan you will need one or two basic items. First you must find a certain amount of money to spend on the materials you will require. Look upon it as a real investment. Your bank will usually grant a loan if you clearly indicate to the Manager that you want the money for home improvement, and you may have a claim for income tax relief on the interest paid.

You will probably ask, 'Can't I get an Improvement or Standard Grant from my local council?' The answer is 'Yes', if your present home lacks the essential amenities of a proper bathroom, hot and cold water supply, inside lavatory or kitchen sink, or mains water supply.

It is not my intention to go into detail in this matter but you can get from your Council Offices a booklet *Money to Modernise your Home* free of charge which sets out clearly what you can expect to get from a sympathetic council. There is also a booklet available from your Council Offices or the Department of the Environment called *House Improvement and Rents, a Guide for Landlords and Tenants* which sets out quite clearly how the 1969 Housing Act works. I also recommend *Improve Your Home on a Grant* by Robert Tattersall, recently published by Stanley Paul at 75p.

However, normal house improvement grants are not given for

Where there's a shell there's a home. An almost derelict property is given a new lease of life with a Marley roof and vinyl cladding. But this is not all. See next page.

Transformation Scene Two, a splendid example of modernisation
brought about by careful planning, patience and the use of the right
materials. The transformation continues on the next page.

As it was in the beginning and as it is now—splendid modern centrally heated, rebuilt from a wreck. A striking example of what can be done.

home improvements and that is what we are concerned with here.

So in addition to some money, you need a notebook and pencil and together we will take a walk round your present home and see what we can do to improve it. But before we do so look at the four photographs on the previous pages. They show a country property in a shocking state of disrepair and some damage caused by bombing during the war. The interior scenes would daunt even the most optimistic house repairer who would probably think the only way to deal with it would be to bulldoze it out of existence.

The roof has been retiled, new windows have been installed, vinyl cladding gives the exterior upper half a distinctive, decorative and protective finish, the faulty corner has been rebuilt and the interior improved to the highest possible modern standard. Central heating has been installed, yet the country house style has been tastefully retained. The old scullery extension has been turned into a modern labour-saving kitchen. What a transformation! Here is Phoenix risen from the Ashes which any man would be proud to own.

This is, of course, one of the outstanding successes of house-rebuilding brought about by a man who had a final picture in his mind, could call upon the assistance of understanding builders and who was able to do a great deal of the work himself. But above all else it shows what can be done by patience and perseverance and is the greatest inspiration to everyone who wants to improve his property.

When you look at your own house and see the jobs which may have to be done and think they are beyond your skills—or capacity to get them done—take another long look at these pictures. They may give you the inspiration you need.

All manufacturers' products and techniques described on the following pages are subject to constant revision and improvement, and intending purchasers should refer to the manufacturers' current literature.

(2) Working to a plan

Now you have decided to take a critical look at your home and are eager to get to work improving it; a good plan is to sort out the jobs which need urgent attention from those which can be tackled later when funds and time can be found.

But always keep in mind that any work done now will be better—and cheaper—than work left when prices are bound to rise. So take a very critical look *now*, noting all the items which could be improved and you can sort them out later.

As first appearances are all-important, start with your front door. Here, more than almost anywhere else, you can tell whether the rest of the property is cared-for or neglected. If it is in bad condition with shrunken panels, botched up with many coats of paint it has no place in the new home you are going to create.

As you can get a new exterior door for £7-£8*, and fitting it is no great problem, why not make a start here? Fixing a door and erecting a porch will be discussed in a later chapter; meanwhile we'll put it down in your notebook.

Naturally the hall calls next for attention. Is it a bright, cheerful, welcoming place? Is the lighting right? Can you introduce a little more daylight? Would the use of mirrors give it the impression of being much larger? Is the ceiling bright and clean, the wallcoverings in good order? And what about the flooring? Isn't it time you had a change? That old floorcovering has probably been down for years and for a very small outlay you can immeasurably improve first appearances by the use of a modern, decorative, easy-to-clean vinyl in tile or sheet form.

However, tradition decrees many people prefer hall and staircase to be close carpeted, giving a quiet, walk-on surface which is warm and decorative. Plain wall-to-wall carpeting gives the impression of more space and it is a simple enough job to lay with a wide range of flooring accessories such as carpet

* The prices given in this book are correct at the time of going to print but do not include any V.A.T.

grippers and cover strips carried in the specialist DIY shops.

Full-width stair carpet should be fitted to prevent accumulation of dust in the corners and the new types of tackless stair grippers allow you to make a very neat and close-fitting job. The big merit of these fittings is that you can take up the staircarpet and move it up or down to minimise wear in one section.

You will probably want to do a repainting job too and here, of course, your choice will almost surely be a top quality brilliant white gloss paint, long-lasting and easy to clean.

Is the hall a cold one? Think about extra heating, too, for whether your hall is tiny or huge it is a place of welcome and should set the tone for the rest of your home.

If your home is on more than one level take a critical look at your staircase. Could it do with a face-lift? There's much to be said, in spite of open plan treads which are dust traps, for some infilling of the balusters which, painted white, make the whole staircase contribute to the brightness of the hall.

Now consider the doors leading to the various rooms. Are they up to the standard you are hoping to achieve? Here again the advice is: repaint or replace. Good quality interior doors can be obtained much more cheaply than you imagine. Take a critical look at the range available in the specialist shops—£3-£4 each is surely something to consider.

If there's one room in the house where a little effort can pay such rich rewards, especially if the lady of the house spends much time in it, it is the kitchen. A whole book could be written on this subject but everyone is familiar with the fabulous kitchens illustrated in all the glossy magazines. These pictures, which never show the side from which the pictures are taken (as many are merely studio set-ups) often look enormous and you dismiss them as being far beyond your reach. But don't despair. There's a marvellous range of easy-to-assemble units available today—in the next chapter they will be dealt with in detail—and you will be sure to find something which will transform your out-of-date kitchen into a modern one.

So into the notebook put: replan kitchen to a modern, labour-saving standard.

Bedrooms are next on the list and here the recommendation must be to give yourself more air and space. That means changing over from the cumbersome free-standing furniture to built-in units. Chapter Six describes what is available and how to set about a new bedroom scheme.

HOME IMPROVEMENT PLAN

FRONT ENTRANCE
Repaint front door to a first class mirror-finish standard. Consider replacing it if woodwork is past repair. Think about a weather porch and garage.

HALL
New carpet or vinyl flooring. Repaint woodwork, doors, undercoat and top finishing coat. Consider new light fitting. Try different positions of large mirror(s). Think about ceiling and wallcoverings. A storage heater for a cold hall, or an extra loop and radiator in the central heating system?

STAIRCASE AND LANDING
Repaint, or if you prefer it, strip, stain and varnish natural woodwork. New stair carpet to give a new look? Repaint in lighter colours all doors leading to upstairs rooms. Fix a loft ladder to give easy access to water supply and loft space. Insulate the attic after clearing out all unwanted items. Check lagging on all water pipes. Fix a new insulation jacket to the hot water tank in the airing cupboard.

KITCHEN
Examine new kitchen units. Recover floor. Consider area of wall tiling and replacement of old white 'hospital' tiles. Provide more socket outlets. Fit new sink unit and replumb with modern polypropylene waste traps and waste systems.

BEDROOMS
Look at new types of built-in fitments. Consider re-decoration to complement them. Install vanity unit and plumb to waste and supply systems.

BATHROOM
Re-tile walls. Consider new bathroom suite now the prices are so low. Examine advice—given in later chapters—on how to fit it up yourself. Get new bathroom cabinet. Fix shower. New flooring to complete scheme. Fit new taps and accessories.

SITTINGROOM/ LOUNGE
New fireplace? Double glazing? Make units for books and hi-fi systems?

EXTERIOR WORK ON HOUSE
Must replace dangerous and leaky cast iron guttering. Do re-pointing of bad brickwork. Consider refacing areas with PVC Shiplap.

EXTENDING THE HOME
Think about home-extension. Make a covered way. Get a shed/workshop, garage or carport.

AROUND THE HOUSE
Paths, paving, fencing, walling. Must look at each section.

GENERAL
Get leaflets, work out prices. Order first materials.

You may now think, how am I going to set about all these jobs being described? Have patience, all will be made clear.

There is a logical order to all these things. You make your notes to begin with, you consider carefully what constructional work must be done first and then you concentrate on the decorative side. It is a comprehensive plan but you can call a halt whenever you like, for there are other parts of the home to consider too—perhaps a home extension, a garage or a carport, perhaps a covered area, a greenhouse maybe, for the garden area around your house is very much a part of your home.

Be a better painter

Before you start any painting job it is a good idea to reflect upon the amount of effort which has gone into producing the paint you are about to use. The leading manufacturers spend vast sums in research and development designed to produce the very best product for the money.

Quite obviously to get the best results from it you should follow the manufacturer's instructions for they know all its merits and its limitations.

The one basic factor needed to achieve the finest result—a finish equal to that produced by a craftsman—is to ensure that the surface to be painted is *suitable.* This means that it must be clean, dry and free from loose material. And it should, in most cases, be as smooth as possible, free from pits and cracks.

Accept the fact that success in painting any surface depends upon 75 per cent preparation and 25 per cent finishing, but this does not mean that you have to strip off any paint which is still in sound, but faded, condition.

Only when a surface has many blisters, flaking paint or cracks is it necessary to put in sufficient work to provide a suitable surface. What does 'suitable' mean? And how much paint is needed for a particular job?

I think the simplest answer to both questions, especially since the paint industry has adopted the metric system, is to base it on figures issued for professional decorators, originally compiled by the Paint & Paint Industries Liaison Committee and published in the March 1972 edition of the technical journal *Painting & Decorating.* The figures quoted are practical ones for brush application, achieved in large scale painting jobs and take into account losses and wastage, but it is emphasised that the figures could vary by approximately 15 per cent either way depending upon the absorbency, unevenness of surface to be

16

painted, choice of colour, and temperature at the time of application. (See pages 18 and 19).

The basic starter-kit required for the competent re-decoration of a house is this:

Brushes. 1in. for fine work, 2in. with a thick head of bristle to carry a fair amount of paint, a 5in. wall brush for emulsion paint. Many amateurs have forsaken the brush for the paint-pad as they find they are easier to use, cover larger areas at one stroke and are extremely useful for emulsion paint. If this is your choice get the complete outfit, one with replaceable pads. There are also many other gadgets worth considering: for example a self-priming roller from a pressurised container, a

Many amateur decorators find the new types of pad brushes easier to use than standard brushes particularly where large areas of wall or ceiling are coated with emulsion paint. The mohair pads are replaceable.

Average coverage of paints in square metres (& square yards in brackets) per litre.

Note: 1 litre is equal to just above 1¾ pints. There are just over 4½ litres in one gallon. A standard 5 litre can contains nearly 9 pints, i.e. 1 gallon & 1 pint.

PAINT TO USE	SURFACES TO BE PAINTED			
	Wall Plaster	Exterior Rendering	Brick Work	Hardboard
WOOD PRIMER OIL-BASED	–	–	–	–
ACRYLIC PRIMER	–	–	–	–
ALUMINIUM PRIMER	–	–	–	–
METAL PRIMER	–	–	–	–
PLASTER PRIMER	11.0 (13.0)	7.0 (8.5)	5.5 (6.5)	–
UNDERCOAT	*	8.0 (9.5)	7.0 (8.5)	*
GLOSS FINISH	*	11.0 (13.0)	10.0 (12.0)	*
GLOSS THIXOTROPIC	*	8.5 (10.0)	8.0 (9.5)	*
EMULSION PAINT	13.5 (16.0)	10.0 (12.0)	8.0 (9.5)	13.5 (16.5)
TEXTURED PAINT	◁ Figures available from manufacturers owing wide variety of types. About 8 sq. yds.			
EXTERIOR PAINTS AND COATINGS		◁ Figures available from manufacturers ▷		

Note: The figures given for Gloss Thixotropic have been provided by manufacturers and the author has rearranged and modified them slightly to make them more easily understandable.

Where asterisks (*) have been used the paint is suitable for the surfaces indicated after any necessary primer or undercoat has been applied.

No figures have been given for textured paints and exterior coatings as there are many different types and no general estimate is possible.

ft ulation ard	Asbestos Sheets	Metal Sheets	Softwood Timber	Primed Surfaces	Smooth Undercoated Surfaces
—	—	—	9.0 (11.0)	—	—
—	—	—	10.0 (12.0)	12.5 (15.0)	—
—	—	—	12.5 (15.0)	—	—
—	—	12.0 (14.0)	—	—	—
—	8.0 (9.5)	—	—	—	—
0 .5)	*	*	*	12.0 (14.0)	12.5 (15.0)
).0 2.0)	*	*	*	*	12.5 (15.0)
0 .5)	*	*	*	*	9.0 (11.0)
0 .5)	12.0 (14.0)	—	*	13.5 (16.0)	*

To achieve a high class 'mirror' paint finish on exterior doors you must build up a good foundation of undercoat before the top finish is applied. It is better to remove all the door fittings so that a full sweep of the brush can be used.

Redecorating walls and staircases can be quite a problem with ladders and boards but a scaffolding kit makes the job perfectly safe for painting and particularly paperhanging where a long 'drop' of paper must be hung.

paint-roller on an extendable arm with which you can experiment if you feel like simplifying matters.

Roller paint outfit. Get a lambswool type as the sponge roller type is inclined to spatter the paint if undue pressure is used and is a bit messy and wasteful when you want to clean it after using gloss paint. However it scores on price.

Paint-stripper, brush cleaner, cellulose filler (there's a new fine surface filler which is most useful in filling chips and deep scratches in paint work and saves a lot of rubbing down), *stripping or filling knife* for removing old wallpaper, *abrasive paper* (wet and dry) and various grades of glass paper, *paint cleaner* for wiping down grubby gloss surfaces or gloss-painted woodwork.

Additionally, some means of getting close enough to the work so that it does not involve any undue physical strain, i.e. stepladders, platform steps, or one of those indispensable tower platforms which make both interior and exterior work simple.

If you consider that the purchase of such a tower is not a good investment remember you can hire one at very moderate cost.

No attempt is made here to provide a complete treatise on repainting but the following simple hints may help.

There is no need to strip off any surface which is sound and holding well. If it is old gloss paint, wash down and lightly sandpaper to remove the shine.

Use the undercoat specified for use with the finishing coat. This is especially necessary when you are using modern, bright colours. You can apply gloss coat over old gloss paint and emulsion paint but if you intend to use emulsion paint over old gloss paint you must ensure that it has a good 'key'. It may prove better to use one of the new vinyl emulsions.

If exterior paint is really bad it should be removed. Try to do this during a spell of dry weather for once the woodwork gets damp you must wait for it to dry out otherwise blisters are inevitable. For outdoor work removal of old paintwork is better done with a modern, safe blowtorch. It is immediately ready for use but you must keep the intense flame moving steadily ahead of your stripping knife to prevent scorch.

Don't allow flaming droplets of paint to fall. Keep plenty of old wet rags available to wipe off the debris from your knife. Don't use a blowlamp unless you have a sure footing and are prepared for any emergency which may arise.

If you have any doubt use a chemical paint stripper and follow the instructions carefully. And if the use of a chemical gives cause for alarm the only other alternative is to use a scraper or power sander.

Tools for the home improver

No practical man can hope to cope with the 101 jobs around the house without an adequate collection of first-class tools. If you intend to follow some plan for modernisation of your home necessitating structural alterations and additional built-in fitments you must expect to get together a comprehensive range of equipment with which you can do all your various jobs with the minimum expenditure of energy and inconvenience.

As time is always a precious commodity it is quite obvious that the right blend of power and hand operated tools is most important. For the beginner who has had no training in the craftmanship of woodworking handtools the power-operated type has a distinct advantage in many respects, for once they are correctly set-up they are capable of precision repetition work of a high standard.

It will be as well at this point to consider how and where the tools are to be kept, for that, in a way, governs the type of tools to buy.

For the flat-dweller with limited storage space who has only a kitchen table upon which to work, and where the noise of power tools might constitute a nuisance, a basic handtool kit ought to consist of the following items.

Claw hammer, about 16 ounces. Make sure you get one with the head securely fastened upon a well-shaped ash or hickory handle. This is a good general-purpose hammer. Ask for size 2.

Handsaw. Get a good general-purpose type, 26in. and see that the blade is firmly fixed, the handle of good shape to fit your hand, the teeth sharp and of a good 'set'.

Tenon saw or backsaw. This has smaller teeth and is most useful for bench work. 12in. size is best for general purposes.

Screwdrivers or turnscrews. One is not enough. Get at least two, three if you can. One should be of a spiral ratchet quick return type as this will save time in driving screws in deep, narrow or awkward places. One other should be about 4in. long and the other at least 10in. Use them only for driving screws! The tips should be flat and not sharp and should fit snugly into the slot of the screwhead.

Brace and bits. A ratchet brace, which permits movement where a full circle of the handle is not possible, is a much more useful tool than a plain brace. They are made in many sizes and types. You will find a 10in. sweep most useful but insist upon one with ball bearings in its head, and with jaws which will take most types of taper shark bits, round shark bits and medium size drills.

Planes. As it is quite a simple matter to purchase prepared timber or man-made board of any size required, a smoothing plane is suggested as suitable here. A number 4 plane, which is $9\frac{3}{4}$ in. long, and has a 2in. cutter is ideal. It is fully adjustable for thickness and unevenness of shaving and will do both fine and coarse work.

Chisels. For most normal carpentry around the house three chisels will be enough: 1in. bevelled edge chisel for paring and one $\frac{3}{4}$ in., and one $\frac{1}{4}$ in. firmer chisel for cutting mortises.

Measuring tools. A 3ft. folding boxwood rule, and a flexible steel rule. A carpenter's square or try-square with a 9in. blade. A 'Stanley' knife with spare blades.

Smoothing tools should consist of a Surform shaper or rasp

for removal of surplus material and a sanding block and various grades of abrasive papers.

Fixing devices must consist of a general-purpose portable vice to fix to a kitchen table or simple workbench, and two 4in. G cramps.

With this basic equipment most of the simple carpentry work can be done quite effectively.

Additional tools you will need for other jobs around the house are: Hacksaw, padsaw and handle, gimlet or push-drill, files (although the shaper type of tool copes adequately with many metalwork jobs), mallet, oilstone and pliers.

Storage of tools

It is most essential to forget the old idea that tools can be stored in a drawer or hung on fittings, however neatly contrived, in a damp shed or garage.

Tools rapidly deteriorate in such conditions in spite of the excellent rust-proof wrapping paper available today. A properly designed tool box or chest is the obvious answer. Each tool should have its right place. Each should be readily accessible without disarranging the others. A correctly designed tool cabinet encourages orderly use and tidiness in putting them back in their proper place when you have finished with them. Toolkits of this type can be readily obtained today.

Having obtained the basic tool kit, you will need something to work on and room to work. You don't have to have a fully equipped workshop before you make a start.

But it is important to remember that in all forms of woodworking, especially sawing and sanding, some degree of mess is inevitable. With a houseproud wife this can be a problem. The rule is: clean up as you go! Put all your tools away and leave the room tidy. The clearing-away job is often the reason why many men never start a job. They want to leave off when they feel they've had enough and can't spare the time to pack away and set up again in the middle of the project.

If you feel like this, then a spare room which you can lock up and keep away from prying eyes, or a workshop in the garden is the only solution, unless you can persuade your partner to help in the clearing up.

A good work bench is really essential if you are to be more than a 'hammer and nails' woodworker.

You need a sturdy top, strong vice and sharp tools if you are to produce satisfying and long-lasting work.

Using power tools

According to research there is at least one electric drill in every household in this country but it does not mean that each one is used with any regularity.

However there is no doubt that the busy home-improver will find a suitable electric drill, with a few attachments for it, to be his greatest ally.

If you have a certain amount of drilling to be done, in walls of plaster or concrete, you should invest in a top quality two-speed drill, perhaps one with a hammer fitment which makes drilling holes in tough material a simple matter.

The slow speed is for drilling, but you need the higher speed for sanding, buffing and sawing.

The circular saw attachment is certainly a most useful aid to have if you have shelving to fit, built-ins to make, fencing to cut to lengths, etc., for a sharp, well set saw blade will save you an enormous amount of elbow work.

The saw attachment can be inverted and inset into a work bench where it becomes a most useful saw table to enable you to cut up sheets of chipboard or hardboard much more easily then if held over a saw-horse.

Although the circular saw will do precision work, some means of finishing to a fine surface become necessary. So the practical man now adds a portable sanding disc, which is merely a rubber disc fitted with an arbor which feeds into the drill chuck. A flat metal sanding plate on which a sanding disc is fixed by an adhesive is used for bench work in a drill press. Or there is a drum sander—a continuous strip of abrasive round a foam rubber drum which makes all sanding work much easier.

If much precision drilling work is to be done in metal, plastics and wood (and perhaps mortising in the latter), a vertical drilling machine is a useful accessory and if there is a need for turning articles such as candlesticks, table legs, eggcups, etc., it is quite a simple and inexpensive matter to add a few bits and pieces to put together the necessary lathe, powered by the electric drill.

It will be appreciated that a power tool workshop can be built up gradually dependent upon your finances. But buying a complete home workshop at the start is probably the better plan, particularly when hire purchase facilities enable you to pay by instalments. In this way you get all the equipment you want at the start and very often something is 'thrown in' as a bonus.

It is, of course, most important always to bear in mind that every safety precaution must be taken in using power tools. They must be kept locked up, they must be electrically sound and no risk must be taken with dangerous electrical hook-ups.

If the equipment of your choice states that you must use three-core cable and proper earth, do see that it is an effective earth. If you are using double-insulated power tools which do not require earthing it is still important to see that your wiring to a suitable point is safe.

Working with power tools requires special care. Loose clothing and dangling ties can be dangerous. Working when you are tired or in a careless frame of mind invites trouble. Circular saw blades should be protected by adequate guards and a push stick should always be used as the end of the work approaches the rotating blade.

For your outdoor work you may need a cold chisel, a bolster chisel to remove faulty rendering, a club hammer and a couple of trowels—a small one for repointing.

A simple hawk to carry the repointing mortar can be made from a 10in. square of chipboard or $\frac{1}{2}$in. plywood to which a 6in. length of 1in. broom handle can be secured.

A metal wheelbarrow makes a useful container for mixing up small amounts of the various Marley mixes but it should be washed out carefully after use and before the residue has set hard.

For work entailing the use of standard building equipment —small concrete mixers, scaffolding, floor sanders, concrete breakers, scaffold boards, etc.—you should contact your local hire shop.

The addresses are given in the Yellow Pages directory.

③
Improving the kitchen

It is only in the past two decades that architects and builders have given any attention to kitchen planning, which means that in most older houses the area spared for a kitchen is nearly always too small to cope with the requirements of modern living.

Today it is the house, bungalow or flat which features a modern kitchen or kitchen/diner, or a superbly fitted kitchen which is most likely to attract the discriminating purchaser.

What can be done to bring yours up to date? The possibilities are almost limitless—only dependent on how much work you are prepared to do and how much money you can spare.

While some present kitchens are awkwardly shaped and small, often needing considerable structural alteration, there is still much you can do to win some extra space without incurring major building costs.

It has probably never occurred to you that a normal hinged door swung back to almost full opening takes up nearly 10sq. ft. of floor space. Even if you open it to right angles, 5sq. ft. of valuable space is lost.

This is where Space-Saver doors come into their own. There is one to suit almost every kind of situation and colour scheme. Eleven colour-ways are offered. Simplest of all is the Foldaway, made of rigid PVC planks, size 30in. × 78in. It runs smoothly in a PVC track and stacks away neatly. The magnetic catch and decorative handle give finger-tip control. It has six folds stacking back to 6in. and installation is simple. If your door height is less than 6ft. 6in. the Foldaway can be cut down to a smaller size.

The popular choices in the range are the Regal and the Wall-Door. The Regal is available singly or in pairs and has a unique pantograph mechanism which ensures smooth action in a U-shaped track and regular pleats of precision made vinyl-covered hardboard panels. It is available in 6ft. 6in. and 6ft. 8in. heights and in widths from 2ft. 3in. to 8ft. An 8ft. high model

27

The opening into which the Space-Saver is to be fixed should be exactly rectangular, plumb and square; and preferably lined with timber of sufficient thickness. The width of the timber lining should be 6" minimum, but if at the rear of the door there are no obstructions, e.g. shelves etc., then 4" width is adequate. The screws should never be fixed to brickwork or plaster by plugging. Always fix to a timber frame. If the opening was previously used for an 'ordinary' door, it is advisable to remove existing door stops.

THE SPACE-SAVER KIT CONSISTS OF:

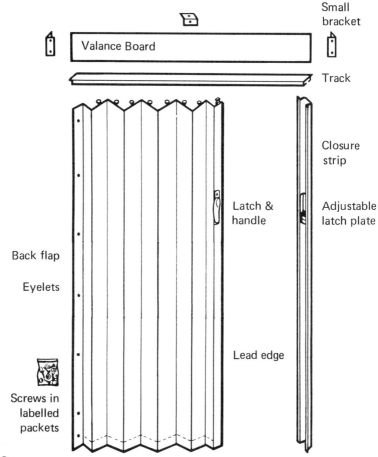

Small bracket

Valance Board

Track

Closure strip

Latch & handle

Adjustable latch plate

Back flap

Eyelets

Lead edge

Screws in labelled packets

is also available. It makes an excellent room divider. The mechanism is concealed by the vinyl-covered valance board.

Somewhat lighter in construction but with the same solid look is the popular Wall-Door in similar heights and made in widths up to 6ft. It has Insulcore panels, is covered and moves smoothly in a U-shaped track. This also has a valance panel and full assembly instructions are provided with each door.

Where a kitchen must be part of a dining area or lounge/ dining room it is often useful to have a room divider which will close off one area from another. Marleyglide is an economical folding system on the made-to-measure principle with a maximum single leaf size of 9ft. 9in. wide by 8ft. high. The hide-texture vinyl is available in nine different colours.

A Space-Saver door adds an attractive feature to any room but it is particularly useful where space is limited. The sliding door gives at least 5 sq ft of extra usable space.

Kitchen floors should be not only bright and gay but easy to clean and easy to maintain. Obviously in this area of home improvement Marley is a household word.

The range of floor coverings offered is so extensive that one is apt to get confused as to which type to put down, for at present there are ten varieties of sheet or roll flooring apart from tiles.

When vinyl floorings first appeared they were made from layers of polyvinyl chloride (PVC) laminated together and this method has stood the test of time with some grades.

Subsequent developments in manufacturing techniques have

HOW TO LAY SHEET VINYL FLOORING

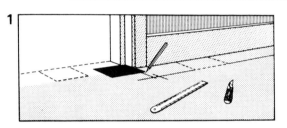

Using Dividers. This can be done even more accurately with "scribers" or "dividers". Lay the sheet about 25 mm (1 in) from the wall, lock the scribers at 6 mm (¼ in) more than the greatest gap between wall and floor covering; hold the scribers vertically and at right angles to the sheet and then, with one point on the floor at the wall, draw the scribers along so that they mark the floor covering with an accurate replica of the wall base line. Cut along this mark. The sheet will then fit snugly against the wall.

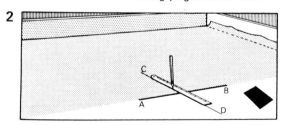

Trimming the Ends. To trim the ends, first draw a check line on the floor along the inner edge of the sheet (*line A-B, Fig 2*). Then, a guide line at right angles to it, on the floor and extending on to the sheet (*line C-D, Fig 2*). Draw back the sheet from the end wall where it over-rides, the excess riding up the other end wall, until there is a gap of about 25 mm (1 in) seeing that the lengthwise edge is along the check line. The guide line on the sheet and on the floor will now have separated (*line C-D, Fig 3*).

Set your dividers or cut a scribing block to this distance. Scribe the profile enabled the makers to spread PVC on felt to form a backed, 'soft to the tread' flooring.

More recent techniques have been developed to incorporate a layer of vinyl foam bubbles between the backing and the top wear surface resulting in what is popularly known as cushioned floorings.

Examples of these stages are Consort and Comfiflor (laminated PVC), Soft-Step and Vynatred (felt-backed) and Fashionflor and Vinylaire (cushioned floor). Comfiflor in fact has a dimpled back which puts it in the 'cushioned' class.

Costwise the range runs like this, starting with Marley

---

of the wall on the sheet, cut and push to wall. The same procedure is repeated at the other end and the whole sheet can be fitted. Trim the ends of the next piece in the same way, but leave the slight overlap of the long edges. The last piece is trimmed against the long wall, and then against the end walls, in the same way as the first.

Double thickness overlap. Now is the time to lose the overlap. Place the straight edge down the length where it covers two thicknesses of sheet, and with a sharp knife cut through the two thicknesses (*Fig 4*). Remove the two narrow cut strips and the sheet edges will fit closely and neatly together.

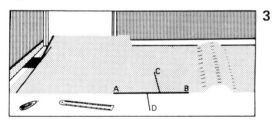

3

Recesses, bays, etc. The same fitting technique applies when trimming the sheet to go into bays, recesses, doorways, or round chimney breasts, etc. The floor covering is roughly trimmed to the outline of the wall, leaving some overlap. Mark the check line and guide line, pull the sheet away from the wall, and scribe and cut as necessary (*See Fig 1*).
Repeat with each irregularity.

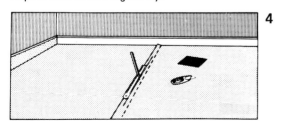

4

Consort at about a £1 per sq. yd. Then there is Soft-Step and slightly higher in price Comfiflor, Marleyflor (1.4mm.), Vinylaire, Vynatred, Fashionflor and Marleyflor (2.0mm.).

Consort, the tough solid vinyl, is available in three widths, 3ft. (0.91m.), 4ft. (1.22m.) and 6ft. (1.83m.) making it the simplest vinyl flooring to lay, while Vinylaire, which has a soft interior sandwiched between a layer of tough vinyl and a backing of Aquacord thermal insulation, is available only in a width of 2m. (6ft. 6in.)

Fashionflor, with its splendid patterns of ceramic tile design, is also supplied in 2m. widths, but because it is of tile design matching the pattern is very easy and there is no waste.

The way to lay sheet vinyl floorings

In pre-vinyl days laying sheet flooring was always something of a problem, for, even with the best types of linoleum, it was not easy to handle quite heavy 6ft. widths of a stubborn material which rolled up at the slightest encouragement and also cracked so easily.

The arrival of vinyl floorings has made the job simple, but in all DIY jobs there's a right way of doing it and the following instructions apply to the well-known types of flooring such as Consort, Comfiflor, Soft-Step, Vinylaire, and Vynatred.

Quite obviously much of the final result depends upon the condition of the floor, whether it be solid concrete, composition, quarry tiles or timber board, i.e. suspended floors.

Solid floors must be dry and remain dry. Any floor showing signs of rising damp, or sweating, must be suspect and the appropriate measures, described on a later page, must be taken.

The floor must be smooth, as all flexible floor coverings take the shape of the floor beneath them and any high spots will soon be visible apart from promoting extra wear in the high areas.

Dry solid floors with pits and uneven areas should be levelled with Marleymix Smoothtex Underlayment. This 'just-add-water' compound is available in two sizes to cover approximately 27sq. ft. or 54sq. ft. at a $\frac{1}{8}$in. thickness. You need a bucket, an old brush and a steel floating trowel.

Having swept the floor clean, removing any old polish or loose material, you should damp down any absorbent surfaces with the brush dipped in clean water. Note that if you have quarry tiles or terrazzo floors you must use a pva primer. Mix the Smoothtex in the bucket, adding powder to water in the ratio

Marley Soft-Step Wood Block. A felt back sheet vinyl flooring which is the most economical cushioned vinyl flooring available.

Simplay International Peel & Stick vinyl floor tiles.

Vinylaire Delphi. A cushioned floor vinyl ▶
flooring in a wide range of colours and patterns.

Consort Peel & Stick vinyl floor tiles offer tremendous scope for
creating your own floor patterns.

Two examples of the attractive and versatile range of home extensions available from Marley Buildings.

Dry, uneven floors should be levelled with the Marley Smoothtex Under-layment to give a smooth hard base on which to lay any flooring. The five stages are simply explained. Use a PVA sealer on non-absorbent floors.

1 Tools required: broom, bucket, distemper brush, steel trowel.

2 Remove all existing grease, polish and loose material and sweep the floor thoroughly.

3 Absorbent surfaces should be lightly damped down with water using a distemper brush. Non-absorbent surfaces such as Terrazzo or quarry tiles should be primed.

4 Mix Marley Smoothtex in a bucket adding the powder to the water, to the proportions of: 3 volumes of powder to one of water. Stir and mix thoroughly until a thick creamy paste is obtained.

5 Pour the Smoothtex mixture onto the floor and spread firmly over the floor using a steel trowel held at an angle. Nominal thickness $\frac{1}{8}$" per application.

of 3 to 1. Stir until you get a thick creamy paste. Pour the mixture on the floor and spread firmly with the steel float held at a slight angle. Aim to get a $\frac{1}{8}$ in. spread. If the indentations are deeper than $\frac{1}{8}$ in. it is better to apply the Smoothtex in two applications, the first drying to walk-on hardness (about 1 hour) before the second coat is applied. No finishing off is necessary as any trowel marks will disappear as the self-levelling action progresses.

The floor should then be left for 24 hours to condition.

Timber floors may need more preparation. It is essential that all loose boards should be secured, any protruding nails punched down, wide gaps filled with a joint filler and proud edges or high spots planed or sanded down.

Remembering that 'the better the sub floor, the better the finished flooring', it is often recommended that hardboard should be used as an underlay. As hardboard must be conditioned with water (one pint applied to an 8ft. x 4ft. sheet and left for 24 hours to reach room humidity) Marley flooring experts prefer 4mm resin-bonded plywood. This is a static material unaffected by moisture. It costs more than hardboard but the initial extra cost is well worthwhile as flooring is a long-term job.

Before laying sheet flooring it should be stored at room temperature to facilitate handling and cutting. Always try to lay vinyl flooring in a warm room.

You will require the right tools: a sharp short-bladed knife or household scissors, ruler or steel tape, a straight edge of metal or wood, scribing block, dividers or a template former. A scribing block can be made from a rectangular scrap of wood.

While a detailed instructional leaflet is available from your supplier the following basic rules show how simple the job becomes.

First plan the layout, deciding which way the flooring is to run to allow for minimum waste and to ensure that any joins do not come in doorways or where traffic is heaviest.

Cut the first length to allow for a $\frac{1}{2}$ in. overlap at each end. Put this down so that there is a similar overlap along its length against the wall. Cut another length, matching any pattern, that will allow an overlap of $\frac{1}{2}$ in. at each end and lay it so that it overlaps the first length by a similar amount. Cover the whole floor in this way although in most kitchens two or even less widths will be ample. With any projections, say a sink unit which cannot be moved, trim the sheet roughly to allow a slight

overlap. Leave the flooring to settle or relax—a few hours to several days will make all the difference to the final result. You can follow the instructions shown in the illustration on pp. 30-31.

It is always advisable to make a permanent fixing of vinyl flooring by the use of the recommended adhesive.

An all-over application of adhesive is recommended and this is done by turning back the vinyl halfway and spreading the exposed floor surface with adhesive. The floor covering is then laid back on the adhesive and pressed down. The process is repeated with the other half of the sheet. Marley recommend that a smooth weighty object should then be 'ironed over'. A bag filled with dry sand is suggested.

Note that for all types of Marley Vinyl, with two exceptions, the recommended adhesive is Marley 118. For Vinylaire and Fashionflor Marley 148 adhesive should be used.

Floor tiles
If beginners feel that the laying of sheet vinyl flooring is a task beyond their capabilities then obviously their problem can be solved by the use of vinyl floor tiles. They make a special appeal for use in smaller areas or where there would be much cutting and fitting to do of sheet vinyl.

Where extra wear of small areas is inevitable, tile flooring, because single tiles can be replaced, makes the repair more economical.

Once again there's a floor tile to suit everyone's pocket and purpose. One of the cheapest and simplest available is Simplay International Peel & Stick 250mm × 250mm (10in. × 10in. approx.), for once your sub floor is prepared and you have worked out a plan of how the tiles will be placed, you simply peel off the backing paper and press each tile into position. It is simplicity itself.

Marley's Peel & Stick vinyl floor tiles are available in three types and a wide range of colours: Consort Peel & Stick, Simplay International in metric size of 250 mm square (approx. 10in x 10in) and Heavy Duty (H.D.).

This young couple may well feel pleased with their Peel & Stick H.D. (Heavy Duty) vinyl floor tiles.

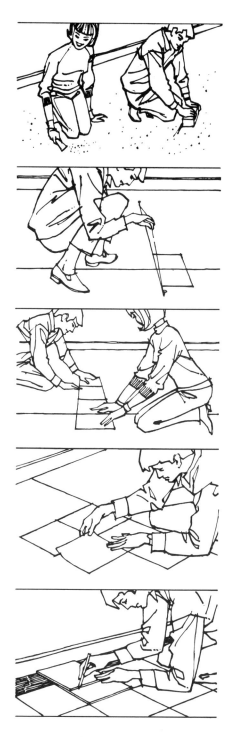

HOW TO LAY
VINYL FLOOR TILES

The pictures show how simple it is to lay floor tiles. The floor must be dry, smooth and firm and brushed clean. Protruding nails should be removed and any high points planed or sanded down. If the floorboards are in a poor condition preparation should be done as described for sheet flooring.

Measure the two end walls and put nails in the floor at their centre points. Tie string tightly from nail to nail and chalk the string. Lift it and let it snap back to leave a chalk line on the floor. Mark the centre of this line, place tiles at each side and draw a pencil line along the edges to make a right angle with the chalk line. Fix a chalked string exactly over this line and snap it. The tiles can now be applied knowing they will be square with the walls. From this point laying the tiles will depend upon whether you choose tiles which require adhesive applied to the floor or the Peel & Stick type which carries its own adhesive. Detailed instructions will be supplied with the tiles.

Marley manufactures a range of vinyl flooring accessories to be used with their floorings. These include a plain skirting where a cove is not required, sit-on cove skirting to give a perfect union with the floor, a set-in cove skirting where a welded floor finish is required and stair nosings for concrete or wooden stairs. There are also flexible edging strips to make a neat, safe edge and feature strips for introducing pattern or design within the floor.

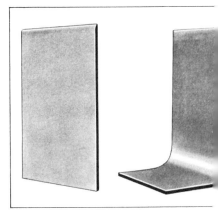

Moving up the range there is Consort and Consort Peel & Stick 9in. x 9in. tiles (229mm x 229mm) in packs containing a square yard but if you are a bit more ambitious you can choose Marleyflor 1.4mm and 2.0mm thick tiles which are 300mm square, i.e. $11\frac{7}{8}$in. x $11\frac{7}{8}$in. There's also Marleyflex International 2.0mm thick, 250mm square and Heavy Duty 2.0mm in 300mm squares. You need adhesive with these. Finally, there is a Heavy Duty (H.D.) Peel & Stick tile of professional quality in a super range of subtle shaded colours which provide an outstandingly beautiful floor.

While this completes a splendid range of floor coverings it is not the end where Marley are concerned for there are many other commercial floorings which are outside the orbit of this book but details are available to anyone interested.

Many newcomers to DIY may not be aware that a range of flooring accessories to be used with vinyl floorings is available and this includes such items as plain skirting, a sit-on cove skirting, stair nosings, stair strings and flexible edging and feature strips, so if you feel you can equal the work of a professional floorlayer get the information before you start your flooring jobs.

Kitchen planning

It is every housewife's dream to have a bright, colourful, labour-saving kitchen where everything is planned to make her daily chores pleasant. Research into kitchen planning shows that in preparing a simple meal a surprising amount of unnecessary lifting, carrying and overreaching is done.

In no other part of the home can improvement be made at a

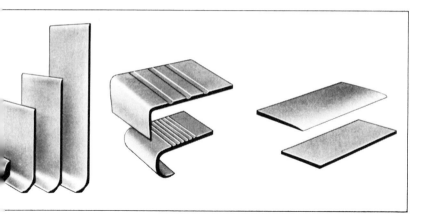

comparatively modest cost and what is so important is that the improvement can be carried out on a DIY basis spread over a period of time and often by extended payments.

The first step is to put on paper details of the present layout, look at the faults, discuss what is needed to bring it up to present-day standards, working to the sizes now offered by manufacturers of self-assembly units on the quick erection principle.

Don't think that plumbing-in a sink unit is a job outside your scope—even that is made simple with the new materials available today and will be explained later in this book.

Manufactureres like Hygena, Be Modern Ltd., and Schreiber have produced a standard range of quick assembly units which merit consideration. Hygena QA sink and work-top units are all at a convenient 35¼in. high with stainless steel tops adding another ½in. They are 21in. deep and work to this same module in length, so you have a single sink unit 42in., or 63in. with double drainer, wall units 21in. and 42in. by 12in. deep. But there are also tall oven-housing and work-top height hob housing units. From this one range the units for a well-fitted kitchen would cost in the region of £140.

The recently introduced Schreiber kitchen units are another attractive self-assembly system of the slot and slide technique without the use of screws and tools. A 42in. base unit can be assembled in 4 or 5 minutes. Sizes are standard in 21in. width modules, 35½in. high and 21in. deep with white Pirelli laminate working surfaces which are fitted with teak-finish bottoms and drawer fronts. There are also matching wall units.

Be Modern Ltd., produce U-Fix units with the simplest

Kitchens to be proud of. Two examples of Hygena Q.A. (Quick Assembly) Kitchen units. A complete range can be seen in Marley centres.

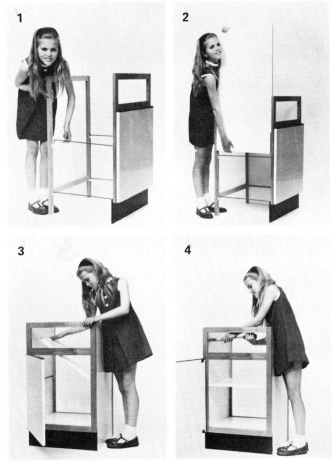

5

6

Assembly of Hygena's Q.A.
units is child's play. This
sequence shows the quick
assembly of a 21 in. base unit.
Tools required? One
screwdriver.

Above: Schreiber Furniture Ltd. make a range of stream-lined kitchen furniture units with the built-in look.

Left: An important feature of the new Schreiber kitchen is the free lift-out rubbish bin inside the sink door.

Below: A feature of the new Schreiber kitchen is a free lift-out, sponge-clean cutlery tray in at least one drawer in each base unit.

possible assembly requirements. You simply take a front section, unfold the side panels, snap the back into place, press the shelves down and screw down the top. Next you screw in the drawer runners, slide in the drawers and that's all. Work tops are in four colours, drawer fronts are all white laminate.

Of course there are many other systems to be seen, for kitchen equipment for the DIY householder is a rapidly growing multi-million pound industry. Everything is being done to make assembly easier and no doubt many new developments now being considered at the time of writing will reach the marketing stage by the time this forecast appears in print.

The kitchen-improver who has some skill in woodwork will probably wish to make his own units tailored to fit exactly the space available. He will doubtless work with Conti-Plas, the white laminate coated particle board in the Contiboard range. Conti-Plas is a decorative laminated board faced both sides and two edges in 6ft. and 8ft. lengths and widths from 6in. to 36in. An eight-page Kitchen Plans book is available from retail outlets for 8p or from Aaronson Bros. Ltd., Church Wharf, Rickmansworth, Herts, WD3 1JD.

With wipe-clean working surfaces and gleaming domestic appliances the rest of the kitchen decor must be in keeping, and this at once suggests areas of ceramic tiling which provides an economical yet permanent form of hygienic decoration. Since the introduction of the $4\frac{1}{4}$ in. x $4\frac{1}{4}$ in. do-it-yourself tile many millions have been successfully applied by the handyman. The confidence they have gained in fixing these tiles to every type of surface—even old tiles—has encouraged them to tackle more ambitious schemes using the mosaic instant-tiles and the new, superbly produced 6in. x 6in. type. The basic technique of tiling will be dealt with in the next chapter.

However, in a book of basic home improvement and particularly when dealing with kitchens, the merits of vinyl wallcoverings cannot be ignored especially by those who feel that tiling is not yet one of their skills.

The techniques for making a first-class job with wallcoverings are described in Chapter Six.

Brightening the bathroom

Once your DIY activities have met with success in transforming your kitchen you will want to follow on in the bathroom and toilet, laundry room or that space which used to have the frightful name of 'scullery'. Many still exist in older houses.

To transform these to the highest modern standard requires a little more effort and some confidence in either your own skills or your ability to persuade a local plumber to do the basic fitting of bath, basin and loo and to leave the rest to you.

When you consider that for about £60 you can get a modern suite of bath in warm, colourful Perspex and a pedestal basin and WC in matching vitreous china you will wonder why you've put up with the present tatty bathroom for so long. And of course, if your present home has no bath or toilet facilities you can claim Improvement Grants from your Local Authority.

Complete suites or separate items are freely available now in most retail shops and often the salesman is able to recommend a local Registered plumber to help you if you feel the task is beyond your ability. His estimate for the work might even take into account an allowance for the disposal of your present bath and sanitary ware.

If you do the job yourself (which may involve breaking up a cast iron bath and disposing of a lot of debris) you must accept that getting everything back into service may take longer than a weekend. And if your present water supply system is supplied through lead pipes which will need wiped plumbers' metal joints or soldered joints to connect up with the new compression or capillary joint fittings you may, and quite rightly, think that this part of the job is best done by someone experienced in this aspect.

However, if you can get this vital part done, the rest is quite straightforward for the waste side of the bath and basin can be very adequately dealt with by the wide range of Marley waste fittings.

Keeping in mind that more and more of the baths on offer

The old and the new. If
your bathroom is old and
tatty like the picture
above it calls for
complete replacement as
shown below. It is
a job within the capacity
of every keen DIY type.

49

today are made of Perspex acrylic and they are therefore very light in weight and can easily be carried by a normal healthy person, and while replacement of the old bath is within your ability, you may still feel that although you want a new look in your bathroom you cannot accept the upheaval which complete reconstruction involves. Only the bath surface is below standard, the rest you can put up with for a time.

There is a bath resurfacing service available by which qualified operators spray on a coating of long-lasting epoxy-resin. This costs in the region of £15, but if you are prepared to go to considerable trouble you can get a new, albeit only comparatively short, life by repainting with a bath 'enamel'.

The surface must be scrupulously clean and lightly rubbed over several times with waterproof abrasive paper (wet and dry), the taps prevented from dripping (small plastic cups can be tied to collect possible drips) and the bath should be warm and dry before applying the first coat. This should be allowed to harden for 24 hours before applying a further finishing coat. If you can wait 48 hours before allowing the bath to be filled with *cold* water, so much the better. Always run sufficient cold water into a repainted bath before letting in the required amount of hot water.

Supposing you have no wish to change your bath and washbasin and are content merely to give the rest a facelift where should you start if there's no major reconstruction to be done?

If there is one job for which the manufacturers have done all their homework it is in the use of ceramic tiles. The whole technique of using these permanent, easy-to-clean tiles has been simplified, whether it be in tiling a plain wall or tiling over old tiles.

The Tile-on-Tile system has encouraged many thousands of men and women to tackle the job with immense enthusiasm and complete satisfaction, especially where the present tiles are still functionally sound but merely crazed and out-of-date in style and colour.

If your present bathroom is half-tiled you can tile over quite simply using the modern Cristal tiles this way.

Make sure the present surface is clean and free from grease. Spread the adhesive with a notched spreader to cover about one square yard with the ridges of adhesive $\frac{1}{16}$ th of an inch high. Press each tile firmly in position but not so hard that the adhesive squeezes through the spacer lugs. When you reach the

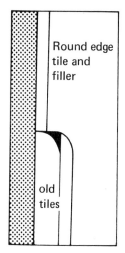

Round edge tile and filler

old tiles

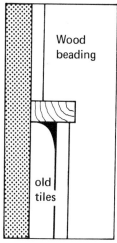

Wood beading

old tiles

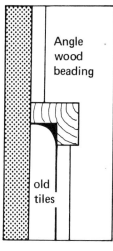

Angle wood beading

old tiles

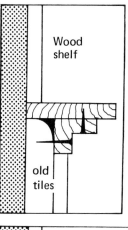

Wood shelf

old tiles

The Cristal Tile-on-Tile techniques. The illustrations show clearly how you can finish off a half-wall stage by the use of hardwood beadings, or by the use of a box shelf, a simple shelf or a feature to carry contrasting tiles in a timber frame.

Fix box shelf to wall and match up with wood beading

old tiles

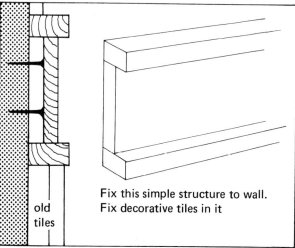

old tiles

Fix this simple structure to wall.
Fix decorative tiles in it

top of the existing half-wall tiling finish off with a row of round edge tiles and make good the gap with a filler. From here you can, if you wish, tile the rest of the wall to the ceiling.

If you want to avoid this obvious cover-up job there are several ways to overcome it.

You can stop at the half-wall stage and finish the step back with a hardwood beading (polished teak is excellent) or use the box-shelf idea as shown in the illustration. Finished examples of this look most attractive.

But if you are starting from scratch on an untiled area, or wish to remove the old tiles (you'll be surprised at how much debris there is), these are the stages to follow (see illustrations on page 54):

1 *Establish a level base.* The surface to be tiled should be reasonably flat and free from dirt, grease and flaking.

If tiling is to be carried down to floor level, first find the lowest point of the floor line, and at this point make a mark on the wall one tile high above floor or skirting board. A lath with a true edge is then nailed to the wall with the top edge up to the mark. Use a spirit level to make sure that the lath is level. Taking this lath as the base line continue nailing laths round the full perimeter of the room (or at least draw a line at this level). This ensures that the tile joints will meet accurately at the starting and finishing points.

2 *Set out the area to be tiled.* The area to be tiled should be carefully set out so that the tiles are used to the best advantage. In this way, very narrow or awkward cuts can be avoided.

The easiest way to do this is to take a lath. Using Cristal tiles for measuring, mark off in tile units (including the spacer lugs) and use the lath as a measuring staff. Set out the wall so that the tiling is centralised, which will leave an equal cut tile at each side. Start at the left-hand one of these points.

3 *Establish a true vertical line.* Having decided on the most convenient point to start tiling, a true vertical line to serve as a guide can be established from it with the aid of a simple plumb-line. Mark the line on the wall in pencil.

4 *Applying the adhesive.* Apply adhesive to the wall surface with a wallpaper scraper over an area of about 1sq. yd. Then spread it with a notched spreader held at approximately 45° to form ridges of adhesive to provide a most satisfactory bed for the tiles.

When working in particularly confined spaces, or with cut tiles, spread the adhesive on to the back of each individual tile, about $\frac{1}{16}$ in. thick.

5 *Positioning of tiles.* Starting at the intersection of the horizontal and vertical laths, begin with the bottom row of tiles and work upwards. Press each tile firmly into position. Do not slide the tiles or the adhesive will squeeze up through the joints. You will find that the built-in spacer lugs on the edges will keep the tiles evenly spaced apart, ready to receive the grout at a later stage.

As tiling proceeds, both the horizontal and vertical lines should be checked at intervals with the spirit level to ensure that 'creeping' does not occur.

Supporting laths should be left in position until the main tiling is completed. They can be removed and tiles cut to fit the spaces left blank.

6 *Cutting the tiles.* This is a simple operation. It is important to cut through the glazed surface slightly by scoring with a tile cutter. Place a matchstick under and along the scored line and press the edges of the tile sharply and firmly. The tile should snap along the line. A tool which makes the job simple is the Oporto Tile Cutter which has three cutting wheels and handles shaped like pincers. When the anvil part is centred on the scored line the handles are squeezed and the tile breaks cleanly. It is well worth the cost of about £1.20 to make the job of tile and glass cutting so much easier and so much more certain.

7 *Grouting.* Grouting should not take place until at least 12 hours after the tiles have been fixed. Mix the grout to the instructions given. Rub the grout well into the joints with a sponge to ensure complete penetration and a really professional finish. Remove the excess grout with a damp sponge.

8 *Tiling around fixtures.* If a sink unit or similar fitting comes within the area to be tiled, the procedure given in section 1 should still be followed and tiling should proceed to the nearest full tile to the fixture with the part tiles cut in later.

A horizontal lath nailed above the fixture will support the tiling. Sink units are rarely level and therefore are unsuitable as a support base from which to start tiling. A lath should be nailed to the wall at the nearest tile's height from the top of the lowest point of the fitting. This should be used as the base for the bulk of the tiling.

9 *Tiling around windows.* Be sure to see that there are no narrow or awkward cuts entailed. Tile to the nearest whole tile next to the window opening as for fixtures.

Support the tiling above the window with a lath. After setting (12/24 hours) laths are removed and tiles cut to fit up to the edge of the window opening. If the edge isn't true, tiles should be cut evenly to provide a true edge against which the reveal (round edge) tiles can be fixed.

In many cases an 'L' shaped tile will be required at the corners of the face. Mark off the position of the cut on the tiles. Score with the tile cutter and nip away gradually to size with a sharp pair of tile nippers. Now round edge tiles can be fixed on the reveals, care being taken to match up to the joints of the main tiling.*

Use pieces of card for spacers as you will have removed the spacer lugs and you must keep the spaces for grouting evenly. Mitres should be formed at the internal corners. Rub to shape after cutting the tiles to size.

Soffit tiles (those fixed under a window or doorway arch) will remain in place if firmly pressed into position or they can be held in position with a length of timber or plywood supports.

How to calculate the number of tiles required:

For small areas simply allow three tiles for every 13 inches. This represents three $4\frac{1}{4}$ in. × $4\frac{1}{4}$ in. tiles, plus the size of the spacer lugs which are on the edge of each plain tile to provide an automatic and even space for grouting.

For larger areas use the table on p. 56. Measure the length of the area to be tiled and the depth. Compare your measurements with the table and you will arrive at the number of tiles required.

Fitting a shower

One of the first requirements of a modern home is a shower, not only because it can double the bathing facilities, but because it provides an economical and invigorating aid to personal hygiene at a quarter of the cost of hot water used for a bath.

There are several ways by which shower facilities can be realised but certain basic facts must be considered.

The first requirement is adequate water pressure, normally

---

* Round edge tiles should be fixed on the reveal of openings (the internal side surface of windows and doorways), not on the face of the wall.

Table showing lineal measurement to nearest ½" for estimating quantities of 4¼" x 4¼" tiles with spacers

Ft.	In.	No. of Tiles	Ft.	In.	No. of Tiles	Ft.	In.	No. of Tiles
	4¼	1	4	8	13	8	11½	25
	8½	2	5	0	14	9	4	26
1	0½	3	5	4½	15	9	8	27
1	5	4	5	8½	16	10	0½	28
1	9½	5	6	1	17	10	5	29
2	1½	6	6	5½	18	10	9	30
2	6	7	6	9½	19	11	1½	31
2	10	8	7	2	20	11	5½	32
3	2½	9	7	6½	21	11	10	33
3	7	10	7	10½	22	12	2½	34
3	11	11	8	3	23	12	6½	35
4	3½	12	8	7	24	12	11	36

5

Example: Total length 12 feet, height 8 feet, length needs 34 tiles and height needs 23 tiles. 34 x 23 = 782 tiles. Estimate the number of round edge tiles required by comparing the total length of all places requiring round edges with the table.

Amount of Adhesive Required.
The amount of adhesive required is simply calculated by allowing 1 lb. for every ½ sq.yd. (36 tiles).

Amount of Grout Required.
1 lb. of Tile Grout is sufficient to grout approximately 2 sq.yds. of tiles.

Below: The stage-by-stage of laying tiles on a bathroom floor.

governed by the height of the base of the cold water cistern above the shower sprinkler head or rose. This should usually be about 3-5ft.

The second is to realise that in the normal domestic plumbing system using direct or indirect hot water storage, hot water will be under pressure from the cold water cistern. As the two supplies should have equal pressure the cold water supply to the shower should come from that cistern and not from the mains which would be much higher. The reasons should be obvious. But when the cold water supply is taken from a branch in the cold water supply to a basin or WC there is a danger that if water is being drawn off at either of these sources the cold water supply to the shower will be reduced and the temperature of the shower water greatly increased, with consequent scalding.

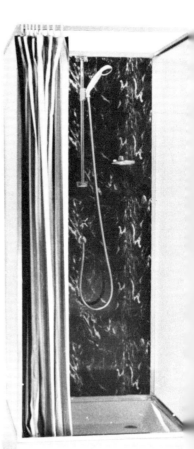

This is one of the drawbacks to the use of the low-priced shower outfits which simply push on to the taps of the bath In spite of this criticism many thousands of these outfits are sold and provided they are used intelligently give complete satisfaction. They are particularly useful for shampooing, etc.

If you propose to fit an overbath shower, screens and curtains will be necessary. The Valba Metlex hinged shower screen, which is 4ft. 6in. high and 2ft. 3in. wide (fixed with four screws) fits to the bath rim and wall and folds back for easy cleaning. You can see several types in the retail shops.

Obviously if you have some spare space available—and you only need an area of 30 inches square—in a bedroom, end of a corridor, on the landing or a disused larder, you can be more ambitious and install a complete shower cubicle and this would cost somewhere around £60-£70, but here again you could economise and be content with a plastic tray or ceramic tile base with a suitable curtain or DIY enclosure. Of course you'll need to fit a modern bathroom cabinet and here it is very much worthwhile to get the best you can.

The Athena range of shower cubicles includes a three-wall cubicle with centre curtain, a two-wall one with wrap-around curtain and a single wall cubicle with wrap-around curtain, so

there's one to suit every position. They can be had in four colours and are $73\frac{3}{4}$in. high, $31\frac{3}{4}$in. wide and $31\frac{3}{4}$in. deep. Supplied packed flat for easy home assembly, they are complete with shower base, waste fitting, chrome plated plastic soap dish and cloth towel rail, curtain and rings and a heavy chrome mixer tap, flexible hose and hand shower.

Almost the final touch to bring glamour to the bathroom is the fitting of venetian or roller blinds. The latter are very much the 'in thing', not only in kitchens where the gay colours can match or complement any special decor, but in dull bathrooms where they produce a really colourful effect. You are bound to find a pattern to please you in the Sunstor roller blind range.

Ordering is a simple matter. You decide whether the blind is to go outside or inside the window recess. Note that the

Two freestanding shower cubicles now in the retail shops. These are the Athena and the Apollo by Porta Showers Ltd.

cloth size is always 1½ in. less than the overall pin size. If fitted inside simply give width and height of the recess, if outside decide how much you wish to overlap at each side and at the top and bottom remembering the 1½ in. difference between cloth size and pin size. Order 'pin size by drop'.

You will see Faber Venetian Blinds in the retail shops. These are all aluminium, completely washable and carry a five year guarantee. Available in a wide range of colours the slats are 1⅜ in. wide (35mm.) and 2in. (50mm.). They will fit all kinds of windows and are easily fixed. The complete blind clips into end brackets making removal for cleaning simple. Another feature is that they automatically lock at any height you choose. A tilting cord makes adjustment simple. An order form in your retail shop shows how you should order, for these refined blinds are custom-made to your exact requirements.

Nothing adds more to a face-lift in the bathroom than the use of colourful accessories such as towel holders, toothbrush holders, new taps and bathroom furniture. There's a wide choice available today.

And if there's one thing to give a look of comfort in the loo it is the use of a bright new WC seat and cover.

The Orchid Isle luxury bathroom suite by Shires has many attractive features with the rectangularity of the bath's exterior contrasting with the soft curves and contours of the interior. The theme is developed in the design of the other ceramic items in the suite.

(5) Livening up the living room

Most home lovers have very decided views as to what they want in a living room. Some desire almost a clinical look with immaculate decor enhanced by avant-garde furniture in skeleton steel and leather. Others want the other extreme—a cosy, warm look of Victoriana with an amount of modern comfort.

But there is a common denominator in that each is a living room where entertainment and relaxation is possible coupled with the minimum demands on maintenance and labour.

This means that ceilings, walls, flooring, lighting, soft furnishings and furniture should fit the total decor.

The essential need in most living rooms is for more space and that requirement can best be satisfied by the use of built-in fitments and shelving systems to accommodate some of the free standing and space-consuming items.

Recently introduced is a complete KV decorative shelving system in a variety of styles which will transform any wall. The high-quality aluminium or steel standards are screwed to the wall while brackets in matching metal are slotted in and given a gentle tap to close the patented locking device. The aluminium type is available finished in walnut, gold, black and natural, while the steel type is available in Statuary Bronze, Satin Anochrome, Antique English, Stain Brass and Aztec Silver as well as four new Aquarius colours of Autumn Orange, Avocado Lime, Moonlight White and Citrus Yellow.

A refinement is the addition of solid wood colonnades which fit on the KV shelf standards. Ready-shelf completes the decorative picture with a variety of pre-cut lengths and widths. Get a leaflet from your local retailer which describes the whole attractive system in detail.

As no two rooms are quite alike the home-handyman will want to build his own and unless he can put his hands on a supply of suitable timber at low cost he will make use of the veneered man-made boards freely available at moderate prices in the retail shops.

Shelving units are the in thing in modern living rooms. The KV shelving system is new and has exclusive features of tap-in-to-lock brackets in a wide range of colours and finishes.

All kinds of units and shelving systems can be built quite simply with one of the types of Contiboard—the veneered chipboard faced both sides with two long edges and sanded ready for use. This is available in 6ft. and 8ft. lengths and widths of 6in., 9in., 12in., 15in., 18in., 21in., 24in., 27in., 30in., 36in. and 48in. Thickness is 17mm. The types available are Natural Mahogany, Whitewood, Teak and Oak but there is also Contiplas, a laminated chipboard with a hard Melamine surface in white or teak grain in similar dimensions but with a maximum width size of 36in. Thickness is 15mm.

Self-adhesive cover strips to be applied with a warm iron are available for the cut edges and boards may be joined with Contijoins—the system of knock-down fittings which make assembly or re-assembly a simple task.

Designs for dining room sideboards, room-dividers and seating units, bench seat units, bookcase, stereogram and bar unit are clearly set out in a splendid 52-page colour booklet available from your retailer at 25p. Bedroom and kitchen units are also featured.

As the sitting or living room is the one most frequently used it must be kept at an even temperature and economies in heating costs can be effected if attention is given to the heat losses which occur through windows, ceilings and floors.

Living room ceilings, no matter how carefully painted, are subjected to discolouration by moisture-laden air, tobacco smoke and the mere act of respiration and it is in this room, perhaps more than any other, where the use of decorative expanded polystyrene ceiling tiles can be used effectively.

Apart from being an easy way to cover cracked and unsightly surfaces they form a pleasingly symmetrical pattern, reduce condensation and have high thermal insulation. And they are very easy to fix.

Several distinct types in a size of 12in. × 12in. × $\frac{5}{16}$in. are available.

The New Regency has 36 2in. embossed squares, the Celestial has a satin sheen of dimpled white, while the Celebrity has a subtle check pattern of 3in. squares. There is in addition an embossed tile (also available in 24in. squares) and Marleycel ceiling tile in three sizes of 12in. × 12in. and 24in. × 24in.

Fixing instructions are very simple. Tiles should only be applied to structurally sound dry surfaces such as plaster, plaster-board, wall board or plywood. Remove all grease, loose paper and dirt from the surface. Loose paint or any material which is flaking should be scraped off. Gloss paint or egg-shell finish should be scored all over by wire brushing, the use of coarse glass-paper, or a scraper such as a hack-saw blade. When this is done, the surfaces should be wiped clean. It should be remembered that adhesive will not permanently bond to dirty or loose, scaly surfaces, and proper preparations of the surface will ensure the best long-lasting results.

To achieve the best effect, it is advisable to measure the dimensions of the ceiling first, drawing a centre line for both width and length. Place the tile face downwards on a clean, flat surface and apply the 124 Marley adhesive to the back of the tile, spreading out with a sweeping motion, using the notched spreader provided, to cover the tile completely. The tiles should then be pressed gently in position within 20 minutes of adhesive application.

Place a group of four tiles around the centre point with two edges of each tile along the line. Keep the edge of the tile exactly on the line to keep rows straight. Place each tile firmly into position using a broad, flat surface to avoid finger indentation. Continue to tile outwards from the centre, keeping the rows of tiles close fitting in line.

The ceiling tiles may be cut to fit with a sharp knife or razor blade at the border and may be left undecorated, or they can be

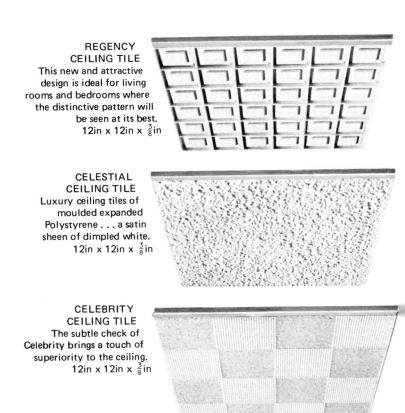

REGENCY CEILING TILE
This new and attractive design is ideal for living rooms and bedrooms where the distinctive pattern will be seen at its best.
12in x 12in x $\frac{3}{8}$in

CELESTIAL CEILING TILE
Luxury ceiling tiles of moulded expanded Polystyrene . . . a satin sheen of dimpled white.
12in x 12in x $\frac{3}{8}$in

CELEBRITY CEILING TILE
The subtle check of Celebrity brings a touch of superiority to the ceiling.
12in x 12in x $\frac{3}{8}$in

treated with an emulsion or water based paint. *Gloss paint must never be used with these tiles.*

It is essential to have clean hands when fixing ceiling tiles.

Marley No. 124 adhesive covers approximately 30sq. ft. per pint.

Finishing off the ceiling with a matching cove is also within everyone's capability. It is light, unaffected by damp and proof against deterioration. Three types can be used depending upon the tile used. The 4ft. x 2in. moulded type is used with Celestial, Celebrity and Marleycel (a cheaper type 3ft. x 1¼in. is similar), and there's a 4ft. x 2in. textured type for Marleycel tiles or general use on a painted non-coved ceiling. Pairs of pre-formed mitres can be obtained to make fixing easy.

If coving is to be fixed to a gloss-painted surface this should be rubbed down or scored to give a key for the adhesive. The coving must not be painted with gloss or oil-based paints.

Cracked and unsightly ceilings may also cause problems of overhead noise and a good deal can be done to combat it by the

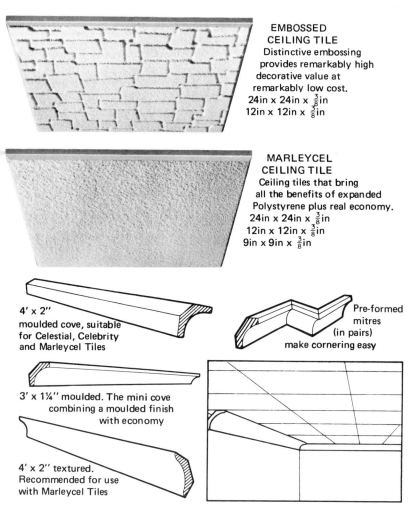

EMBOSSED CEILING TILE
Distinctive embossing provides remarkably high decorative value at remarkably low cost.
24in x 24in x $\frac{3}{8}$in
12in x 12in x $\frac{3}{8}$in

MARLEYCEL CEILING TILE
Ceiling tiles that bring all the benefits of expanded Polystyrene plus real economy.
24in x 24in x $\frac{3}{8}$in
12in x 12in x $\frac{3}{8}$in
9in x 9in x $\frac{3}{8}$in

4' x 2" moulded cove, suitable for Celestial, Celebrity and Marleycel Tiles

Pre-formed mitres (in pairs) make cornering easy

3' x 1¼" moulded. The mini cove combining a moulded finish with economy

4' x 2" textured. Recommended for use with Marleycel Tiles

use of Armstrong ceiling tiles. Some are designed to cope with noise, others are incombustible offering extra protection against the spread of fire. They are particularly effective in older types of property where very high ceilings need to be lowered to reduce heating costs. These 12in. x 12in. tongued and grooved tiles are available in several types, are ready painted, grease proof, with textures and patterns and some have a scrubbable vinyl surface. Others are coloured.

If the ceiling is in good condition, the tiles can be fixed with four walnut sized daubs of Acoustic Cement. Otherwise the tiles must be stapled to battens at right angles to the ceiling joists. A complete instruction sheet is available from your retailer.

Double glazing

Most people are aware of the claims made for double glazing and are repeatedly told that a custom-made system can cut heating costs by a considerable amount. However it is clear that DIY methods make a very great appeal, for even if one is able to reduce heating costs by only 25 per cent and the heating bill is £100 per annum it takes 10 years to recover the cost of an installation on which £250 has been spent.

A very simple system which will commend itself to practical readers has recently been introduced. This consists of a flexible vinyl extrusion designed to clip onto the edge of a 24oz. glass sheet which is then held against an existing wooden window frame by nylon turn buttons. The flexible extrusion acts as a seal creating the vital volume of static air between the two panes of glass. With this new system it is necessary to order glass $\frac{3}{4}$in. larger in width and height than the original window.

Marley Double Glazing System is available in packs containing three 4ft. lengths and four 4ft. lengths to allow you to purchase your requirements with minimum wastage.

Double glazing has another important advantage, it can help to reduce noise. But to be effective as a sound insulator it must satisfy certain requirements: there should be complete freedom from gaps and cracks and the weight of glass is important. Experts say that in well-constructed single-pane windows a reduction in sound transmission of up to five decibels can be

1 Measure window

4 Fit new pane onto window and mark position of turn buttons. The distance between turn buttons should not be greater than 10in.

7 Diagram of corner turnbutton fixing.

obtained by doubling the glass thickness. They prescribe for sound insulation that the gap between the panes should be a minimum of 4in. while 8in. will be more effective. It is also recommended that the lining of the sides of the air space with sound absorbent materials results in greater improvement. Finally it is recommended that for maximum sound insulation rigid coupling between the frames should be avoided and flexible coupling is desirable. Readers who face a severe noise problem from exterior sources might like to note these details. The British Standard Code of Practice gives these figures for levels of noise:

Man talking at a distance of 3ft.: 60 decibels.

Pneumatic drills at 125ft. away in open air: 70 decibels.

Rush hour traffic at 15ft.: about 75 decibels.

Jet-plane at 125ft. passing overhead at take-off: 110-120 decibels.

The Insulation Glazing Association has produced these approximate figures of sound reduction in fixed windows.

Single glazing 32oz. glass: 25 decibels. $\frac{3}{8}$in. glass: 30 decibels. Double glazing 32oz. 4in. airspace: 30 decibels, 8in. airspace: 36 decibels. With $\frac{1}{4}$in. glass the relative figures are 34 and 40.

So if you want both thermal *and* sound insulation these factors should be borne in mind and your double glazing tailored to fit your needs.

2 Purchase new pane of 24oz glass ¾in larger in width and height than window. (max. area 16sq.ft.)

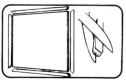
3 Cut and fit vinyl extrusion to new pane, using mitred corners as shown.

5 Hold new pane in place using turn buttons screwed to frame.

6 Exploded diagram of turn-button fixing.

8 Diagram illustrating sealing action of compressed vinyl extrusion.

Marley's new double glazing is a simple vinyl extrusion accepting 24 oz. glass and using turn buttons to provide a seal. Maximum area is 16 sq. ft.

Window condensation

Without double glazing, or sometimes with a simple loose-fitting system, there is considerable condensation on the windows in very cold weather and unless some way of reducing it is found it can lead to serious corrosion of metal frames and the rotting of timber ones.

This is a particular problem when central heating brings about higher than usual room temperatures. Warm air has a greater volume than cold—its molecules are wider apart—and has the capacity of holding more water vapour. When this warm air meets a cold surface 'dew point' is reached, the air becomes cold and shrinks and cannot hold the moisture which condenses on the cold surface.

The simple cure is to open doors and windows so that the room temperature equals that of the air outside but, of course, this is simply wasting your precious warmth.

While extractor fans and ventilators will help, Marley have come up with a simple answer which, although it does not cure condensation greatly reduces its harmful effects on window frames.

Called Window Gutter it is a simple white vinyl extrusion which is fixed on the internal window ledge in contact with the glass. It is shaped to collect any condensation which runs down the window pane and this can be wiped away when necessary. This is suitable in moderate conditions but where there is severe condensation drain tubes can be fitted as shown.

Marley Window Gutter is a white vinyl extrusion which is fixed on the internal window ledge in contact with the glass.

The vinyl extrusion is shaped to collect any condensation which runs down the window pane, preventing it from causing paint damage, decay and mould growth on the wooden window ledge. The condensation collected may either be wiped away when necessary, or drain tubes may be fitted to the gutter so that the condensation is continually piped away to the exterior. The choice of fitting depends on the severity of the condensation experienced. Under moderate conditions e.g. in a bedroom or lounge, the drain tubes may be omitted, but under severe conditions e.g. in a bathroom or kitchen, they should be included.

For moderate condensation conditions, the vinyl gutter is cut to fit the internal window ledge and fixed in place using the adhesive supplied.

For severe conditions, the vinyl gutter is cut to fit the internal window ledge, and holes are drilled through the gutter into the wooden frame to take the drain tubes. Both the drain tubes and gutter are fixed in place using the adhesive supplied.

Diagram 1

Diagram 2

Diagram 3

Severe Condensation Conditions

1 Measure length of internal window ledge.
2 Cut vinyl gutter to fit. If the gutter does not fit snugly, it may be warmed slightly and bent to shape.
3 Position gutter on ledge and drill two $\frac{3}{16}$ in holes 'A' at a slight angle through the gutter into the wooden ledge, about ½in from the ends of the ledge. Care must be taken to avoid glass.
4 On opening lights remove gutter and continue holes 'A' through the window (Diagram 1). On fixed lights, remove gutter and enlarge holes 'A' in frame with a $\frac{5}{16}$in drill (Diagram 2/3). Drill holes 'B' to meet holes 'A' using a $\frac{5}{16}$in drill and continue through to exterior.
5 Feed green tube through these holes (see Diagrams).
6 Insert transparent collars at 'A' and 'B' to take up clearance.
7 Apply adhesive to window ledge and glass.
8 Press gutter into place, carefully pull green tube flush with gutter surface, and trim off excess externally.
9 Remove excess adhesive.
10 Plug internal hole with filler.

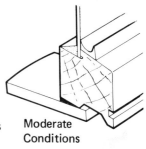

Moderate Conditions

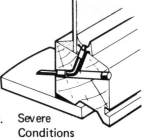

Severe Conditions

The wooden frame and gutter are drilled and the drain tubes fixed with the adhesive supplied.

Readers who have experienced trouble with condensation misting up their double glazing may find that this system can be adapted with advantage.

Furnishing a window with colourful and often expensive curtaining becomes something of a problem in a room where the radiators of a central heating system are inevitably sited underneath the window. If you want floor to ceiling curtaining the radiators are covered up and most of the heat goes out of the window especially if the windows are not double glazed. Even if they are, the concentration of heat in the enclosed area can have a harmful effect on the curtaining material especially if the warm air is trapped at the top in a heavy box pelmet.

If you want to make your full length window curtains a feature of your room—and they certainly can give it height and the impression of width—you should see what can be done to site your radiators elsewhere.

Many experts maintain that heat sources should be placed adjacent to the inner fabric of the house, citing the fact that you cannot place radiators in front of picture windows which run floor to ceiling. Certainly it is true that electric storage heaters which are effective for their even transmission of heat over a long period are never properly sited under windows.

To get full value from radiators installed under windows curtains should be of window sill length only and be fitted with a rail which permits full circulation of air around it.

Some people having installed a plastic rail system and gliders find that the curtains are difficult to pull together. Like all plastics when they are rubbed they develop static electricity which attracts dust making it difficult for the runners to glide smoothly. This common fault can easily be eradicated by wiping the rail over with a cloth dipped in a little liquid detergent.

So far nothing has been said about decoration or floorings and both must play a part in the whole decor. Light vinyl wallpapers and a light wall to wall carpet will give the impression of space; a feature wall area of self-adhesive mirror tiles will give it depth.

If the living room is long and narrow and you need to enclose part while the other part is being used, a luxury vinyl folding partition may be the answer.

These Marleyfold partitions based upon sound engineering

techniques are specified by architects for commercial buildings but are equally suitable for use in the modern house. They are always custom-made and cannot be bought 'off the peg'.

If the living room is large and square the introduction of a colourful pattern vinyl wallcovering with its boldest emphasis halfway up the wall will give the impression of a longer room.

One of the simplest ways to promote a look of elegance in living rooms and bedrooms and especially where walls meet ceilings at stark right angles is to install a plaster-based coving. Until fairly recently this required a fair amount of skill in handling long pieces of gypsum coving and it entailed the use of pins to keep the coving in place while the adhesive set.

With the new Blue Hawk coving the job is very much easier. Now supplied in 2m. (6ft. 6¾in.) lengths with a more powerful Blue Hawk adhesive and filler, even the novice can do a perfectly satisfactory job at a very moderate cost. A template for mitre cutting is provided.

Simpler-than-ever is the new range of ready-pasted vinyl wall coverings. All you need is water, sponge and scissors to apply this attractive Vymura called Clematis.

Another product in the Blue Hawk range will commend itself to every decorator. This is Selftex, a plaster-based plastic compound which not only seals cracks but is a 'paint' finish in its own right, allowing all kinds of textured finishes to be achieved. It sets hard and when dry can be decorated with emulsion paint in any colour you require or left in its original white finish. A 15lb. bucket covers approximately 135sq. ft.

Instructional leaflets are available from your retailer.

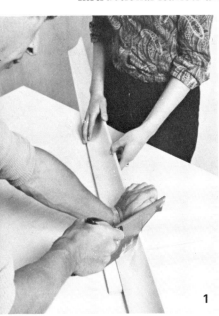

1

A plaster coving adds a look of elegance to any room. The new Blue Hawk coving is easy to install and is now supplied in 2 metre lengths. A special adhesive/filler is supplied. Cutting the mitres is made simple by the provision of a mitre guide.

6

Bedroom built-ins

The basic requirements for a modern bedroom are quite straightforward—a close-fitted carpet, ample storage space for clothes, a double bed or single beds with suitable headboards with drawer cabinets and lights, a dressing table unit which takes up little space and a basin or vanity unit.

Get the best carpet you can afford, a good thick underfelt and, unless you have skill in carpet-laying and are familiar with carpet stretchers and tackless grippers, get it laid by experts. In the long run it will be a little extra money well spent.

Modern bedrooms are made with built-in fitments and here again it pays to choose from a range to which you can add as money becomes available.

The skilled handyman, who has a roomy workshop and can make his own units to fit any particular area and space, will of course, score over the beginner but most new home-owners will find the newer types of quick-assembly units very easy to put together.

The White Space bedroom units by Hygena are typical examples. This is a floor to 8ft. high ceiling system of scratch-resistant surfaces and doors which fasten with magnetic catches top and bottom. A big improvement is that the top cupboard doors open upwards and have lockable stays making it easy to put away out-of-season items. The drawers are deep and roomy, white finish inside and outside and move smoothly on plastic runners.

It is a simple job to work out a combination of units to suit every need. All the wardrobes and top cupboards are 20in. deep front to back. The dressing table, knee-hole dressing table and chest of drawers are 19in. Doors can be hung to open left to right. As well as top panels which can be cut to fit your ceiling height, side filler panels up to 12in. wide are available. Drawers can be adjusted within the wardrobe at two different levels.

The range also includes a linen chest, fitted headboards for single and double bed sizes and these have quilted-effect

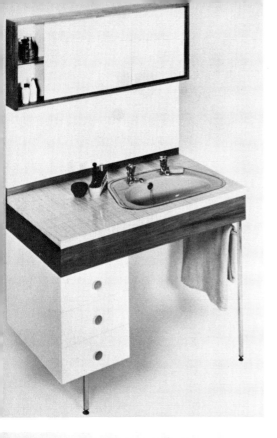

Left: A Hygena Vanity Unit —
ideal for the guest room or
second bedroom or as a feature
in the main one.

Below: The White Space self-
assembly bedroom units by
Hygena are for floor to 8ft. high
ceiling fitting and are based upon
the quick assembly principle.
All wardrobes and cupboards
are 20 in deep. The complete
system includes dressing table,
knee-hole dressing table and
chest of drawers.

oatmeal coloured padding that's easy to keep clean. The continental headboard for double beds has twin drawers, laminate topped. You can see a range of these units in most retail shops and depots.

Ideally every main bedroom should have washing facilities and if the decor is modern a coloured pedestal basin does not look out of place. If you can site this on an outside wall so that the waste can discharge into a convenient hopper the plumber should have little difficulty in connecting up the hot and cold water supplies from an adjacent source. But local regulations of which he will be aware may mean that he will have to connect the waste direct to a soil pipe.

The Marley easy-to-fix polypropylene waste systems for washbasins, sinks and baths are enjoying well-deserved praise from amateur plumbers and professionals and are described in detail here.

The first point to note is that the waste system all works on the push-fit system. No solvents or adhesives are used for jointing. Two sizes of pipe and fittings are available:

32mm. ($1\frac{1}{4}$ in.) and 38mm. ($1\frac{1}{2}$ in.). Pipe is sold in 1.829m. (6ft.) lengths.

The illustration on page 77 shows the range of items and installation procedure.

The waste traps are also sold in similar sizes. All traps have 76mm. (3in.) water seal with ring seal outlet for use with the waste systems.

Many home improvers may feel that the washbasin should be included in a compact vanity unit and this is sound sense if there is space to make a feature of it. A unit made from white Contiplas would be most appropriate in a bedroom fitted with White Space units and there is a basic design with full constructional details in the construction guide mentioned in an earlier chapter.

Before deciding on any design it is important to choose the sort of basin made specifically for this type of unit, and get a template from the manufacturer so that the aperture cut in the surface is exact in every detail.

Decoration of the bedroom should follow any constructional work and this must be left to the individual choice of texture and colour. Generally the effect to aim at is one of restfulness and softness with any splashes of colour provided by bedspreads and scatter cushions. There should certainly be a modest use of ceramic tiles as a splashback area to the hand basin or vanity

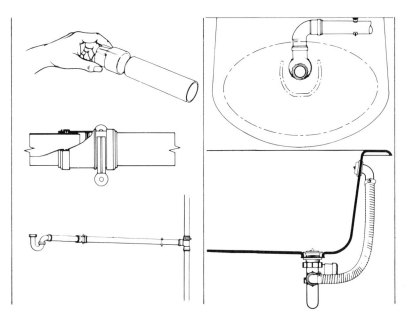

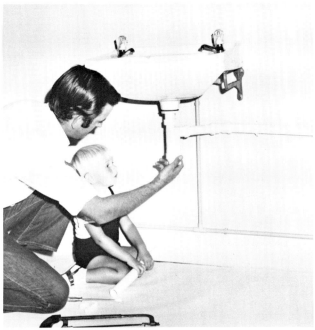

Polypropylene waste systems and waste traps have simplified
the job of fitting handbasins and sink units. All items are
joined by the push-fit method. The full range is illustrated.

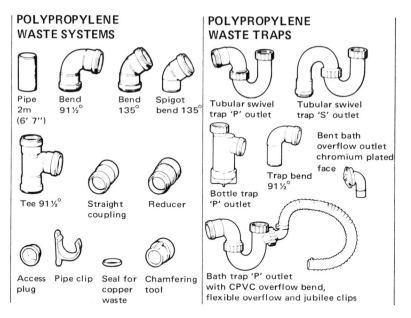

POLYPROPYLENE WASTE SYSTEMS

Pipe 2m (6' 7")

Bend 91½°

Bend 135°

Spigot bend 135°

Tee 91½°

Straight coupling

Reducer

Access plug

Pipe clip

Seal for copper waste

Chamfering tool

POLYPROPYLENE WASTE TRAPS

Tubular swivel trap 'P' outlet

Tubular swivel trap 'S' outlet

Bent bath overflow outlet chromium plated face

Trap bend 91½°

Bottle trap 'P' outlet

Bath trap 'P' outlet with CPVC overflow bend, flexible overflow and jubilee clips

unit. A final touch can be added to take off the squareness of corners, where wall meets ceiling, by installing Blue Hawk cove.

Applying wallcoverings

Improving the decor of the bedroom means that special attention should be given to what is going to be put on the walls and if there is one aspect of do-it-yourself which makes an almost universal appeal to both sexes it is the application of wallcoverings.

Note that last word, for although wallpapers are as popular as ever the word wallpaper is no longer descriptive of the vast range of materials for covering the walls of the modern home.

Just as the types of wallcoverings have changed so, too, have the methods of fixing, with the adhesive tailored to suit the type chosen. It is therefore very important to ensure that they match and this will be discussed later.

In no other sphere of do-it-yourself activity have there been so many trends, improved materials, better designs, ease of application and range of prices than in wallcoverings; a whole book could be written on this subject alone.

But before you consider the types and the uses to which they are most suitable you need to have some equipment and although it is said that you need only a pair of scissors, a sponge and a trough of water to apply the ready-pasted papers, you would be wise to purchase—and the cost is less than £3—a paperhanger's folding table on which to measure and cut your pieces.

For wallcoverings other than the pre-pasted you will need a pasting brush, a smoothing brush, bucket and paste, plumb-bob, sponge, preferably a 24in. metal rule and scissors or shears. With this equipment you will be able to cope with every type of wallcovering.

Stripping off the old types of wallpaper presents no problem if sufficient time is given to the job. It is essential to use enough water to get through the paper to dissolve the adhesive on the back of the paper. This means you must have adequate covering of polythene or old newspapers on the floor to prevent too much mess. If you use a wallpaper stripper which holds the water in contact with the paper you will find the job much easier. Once the old wallpaper is really soaked it is a simple matter to strip it from the wall.

Be careful to hold the stripping knife at an acute angle to the wall to prevent it from digging into the plaster. When all the wallpaper has been removed wipe over the wall with a sponge and rub down any small nibs of paper which may have been left with fine grade glasspaper.

Any cracks in the plaster which may be exposed should be filled with a plaster filler and left to dry out before re-decorating. If you have to remove wallpaper which has been painted with emulsion paint the surface must be scratched to break through the paint. A wire brush will help but a serrated scraper does a better job. If this is not available you can use a broken hacksaw blade fixed into a wooden handle or wrapped round with a duster. The surface is scratched in all directions to ensure that water can penetrate.

Although emulsion-painted walls are popular in most homes, for they are so easy to re-decorate, the surface of many walls, and ceilings too, is so rough that they never re-decorate satisfactorily. In such cases a lining paper should be first applied. Getting a close butt-joint is not always easy with these papers but slight overlaps can be rubbed down with glasspaper 24 hours after the paper has been hung. This is important if you intend to put on another wallcovering. In the latter case the lining paper should be hung horizontally to avoid the possibility of the joints in both papers coinciding.

Woodchip papers have become very popular not only because they are strong papers and easy to handle but because they have

78

an attractive texture which greatly assists in hiding any unevenness of the wall surface. They are effective on ceilings as well as walls and are not so obvious as the earlier type of pebbledash papers.

In bedrooms particularly the newer types of vinyl wallpapers make the greatest appeal for the range of patterns is huge, they are easy to apply and simplicity itself to remove when you want to change them. These are available in pre-pasted forms too and this means that you avoid the sometimes hit or miss method of hand-pasting.

But when you use ready-pasted vinyls you have to cut your pieces almost to correct size before immersing them in water and this means taking a little extra care especially when matching up to an intricate pattern, particularly in corners which may not be true right angles.

There is also another small snag. If you get an overlap (and this is never recommended) the adhesive is not strong enough to hold the paper backing to the vinyl face and it will lift away when dry.

If you must have an overlap it must be secured with a pva adhesive. The alternative to this is to place a steel rule in the centre of the overlap, cut through it with a very sharp knife, lift away the cut pieces and press the mating ends into position. Remember that there is a great difference in technique between applying wallpapers and wallcoverings.

The standard type of wallpapers whether thin or duplex (two thicknesses) should be pasted with standard cellulose or starch-based adhesives and allowed to soak for a few minutes before applying them to the wall.

Heavyweight papers and embossed papers should have a thicker paste applied and should be hung immediately to prevent too much stretching. Where these papers are applied to surfaces 'sealed' by emulsion paint or gloss paint, which has been well-rubbed down to remove the shine, a paste containing a fungicide should be applied.

For the standard vinyl wallpaper a heavy-duty paste should be used and should be mixed exactly to the instructions given on the packet. If you dilute this paste too much you are likely to have trouble with uneven drying out and blisters. Once you have applied the paste, vinyl wallpapers should be hung immediately.

One other point should not be overlooked. When you are ordering any type of wallcovering, especially one with a bold pattern and distinctive colouring, do not underestimate your needs, as if you run short you may not be able to get exactly matching supplies. And when you buy a room-set, say seven or eight rolls, make sure that they are from the same batch of printing. In fact it is better to shade each roll before you leave the shop.

As a simple guide to requirements work to these figures:

CEILING PAPERS

Distance in feet round room 2 x (length + width)	Number of rolls required
30 - 40	2
42 - 48	3
52 - 58	4
60 - 66	5
68 - 70	6
74 - 78	7
80	8

WALLPAPERS

Based upon normal roll of 11 yds. x 20 or 21 inches.

Height in feet from skirting			Rolls of wallpaper required																		
			Measurement in feet round walls, including doors and windows																		
			28	32	36	40	44	48	52	56	60	64	68	72	76	80	84	88	92	96	100
			Number of pieces																		
7	and under	7½	4	4	5	5	6	6	7	7	8	8	9	9	9	10	10	11	11	12	12
7½	" "	8	4	4	5	5	6	6	7	8	8	9	9	10	10	11	11	12	12	13	13
8	" "	8½	4	5	5	6	6	7	7	8	8	9	9	10	10	11	12	13	13	13	14
8½	" "	9	4	5	5	6	6	7	8	8	9	9	10	11	11	12	12	13	13	14	14
9	" "	9½	4	5	6	6	7	7	8	9	9	10	10	11	12	12	13	13	14	15	15
9½	" "	10	5	5	6	7	7	8	9	9	10	10	11	12	12	13	14	14	15	15	16
10	" "	10½	5	5	6	7	8	8	9	10	10	11	12	12	13	14	14	15	16	16	17
10½	" "	11	5	6	7	7	8	9	9	10	11	11	12	13	13	14	15	16	16	17	18
11	" "	11½	5	6	7	8	8	9	10	10	11	12	13	13	14	15	16	16	17	18	18

For the more ambitious home decorator there are many other types of wallcovering which may appeal and these include types of embossed plastic panelling, metallised wallpapers, metallised wall tiles, plastic-faced panelling or timber and plasterboard, cork panels, veneered plywood and photographically reproduced grained panels. Advice on fixing all these types is available at your retail shop.

⑦
Room in the loft ?

No doubt every householder faced with the need for extra living or storage space has said to himself 'Can I use the space in the loft?' Each time he has gone into the attic to check his water storage tank or improved the insulation of the attic he is conscious of the vast void in the roof space. And when he fits a patent loft ladder, as so many do, the easy access prompts him to think of a hobbies room, even a playroom or a bedroom.

But the facts are these. While a normal loft may be used for light storage or occasional temporary use you come up against strict Building Regulations if you propose to build a habitable room. For a storage area a flooring can be put down with tongued and grooved chipboard and this should be screwed down to the joists, but remember that if you cover up your insulation by doing so you will still have a cold storage area. In any case you should have had at least a 2in. layer of insulation material such as Supawrap between the joists or completely covering the floor area, while the storage tank should have been enclosed in lagging materials, the pipes also covered with pipe lagging.

By covering this insulated floor area with chipboard you will, of course, improve the insulation of the rooms below. So if you haven't insulated your loft and propose to fit a floor you can use your insulation material elsewhere say, for example, stapled to the rafters.

So the first point to take into account is that if you propose to build a room in your loft, access by loft ladder will not comply with the Building Regulations—you must have access by a permanent stairway. And you must submit plans to the local authority and await approval before any work is done.

Having decided that there is a possibility of a stairway from an upper room or landing, the next step is to measure up the area of the loft. The essential point here is headroom and the regulations are quite specific. The illustrations are borrowed from a series of four articles published in *Do it yourself*

If you are thinking of a room in the loft you must consider the basic regulation regarding headroom: it must be at least 7ft. 6in. over an area of floor equal to not less than half the area measured at a level of 5ft. above the floor. In the smaller sketch 'W' is the width at 7ft. 6in. over 'W1' the width at 5ft. The large sketch shows how a loft room can be built. Note that if the room is for habitable purposes access to it must be by a permanent stairway.

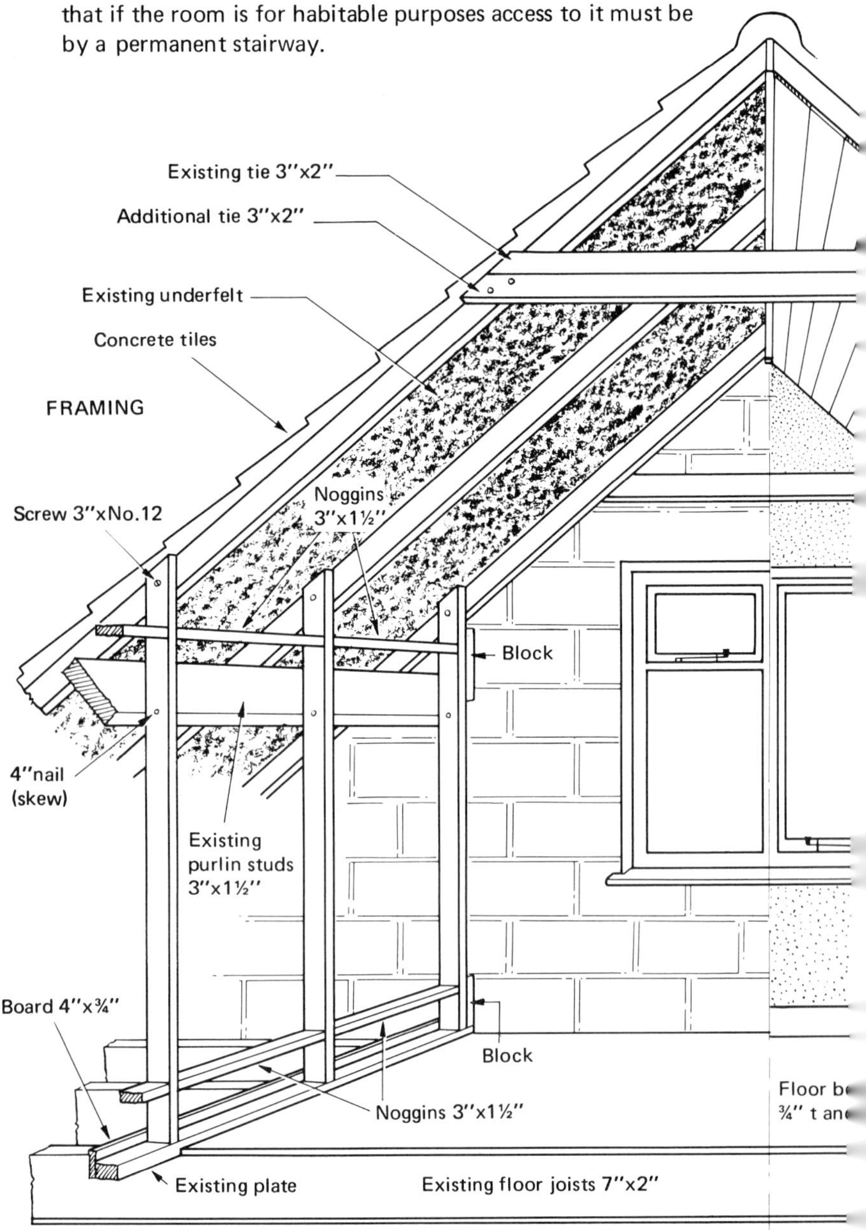

Existing tie 3"x2"

Additional tie 3"x2"

Existing underfelt

Concrete tiles

FRAMING

Screw 3"xNo.12

Noggins 3"x1½"

Block

4"nail (skew)

Existing purlin studs 3"x1½"

Board 4"x¾"

Block

Noggins 3"x1½"

Floor be ¾" t and

Existing plate

Existing floor joists 7"x2"

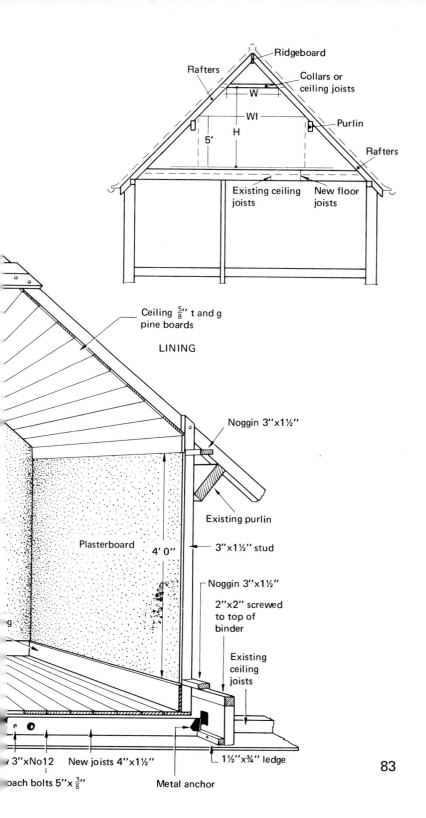

Ridgeboard

Rafters

Collars or
ceiling joists

W

WI

Purlin

H

5'

Rafters

Existing ceiling
joists

New floor
joists

Ceiling $\frac{5}{8}''$ t and g
pine boards

LINING

Noggin 3''x1½''

Existing purlin

Plasterboard   4' 0''   3''x1½'' stud

Noggin 3''x1½''

2''x2'' screwed
to top of
binder

Existing
ceiling
joists

g

3''xNo12   New joists 4''x1½''

oach bolts 5''x$\frac{3}{8}''$

Metal anchor

1½''x¾'' ledge

83

magazine (December 1968–March 1969), and show clearly the requirement.

However even if your calculations prove that you cannot meet this requirement it is not the end of the matter for it may be possible to comply by breaking into the roof and adding a dormer window. A window is an essential part of a loft room as the regulations insist that while it can be of any convenient size the opening part must equal not less than one twentieth of the floor area of the room.

If after careful examination and even calling in the services of a company specialising in loft conversions you find you cannot meet the requirements on cost you can still do quite a bit to make the loft a comfortable place for occasional temporary use.

Flooring must have first consideration. The joists should be examined to confirm that they are in good condition and not attacked by beetle or fungus. If you discover powder by the entrance to small holes you have active woodworm and this must be tackled with a recognised liquid such as Rentokil. This can be brushed or sprayed on liberally, wearing a gauze mask to prevent inhalation of the vapour and making sure you do not spill any liquid to seep through and stain the ceiling of the lower room. Any timber showing fine threads of mycelium of dry rot or fungal growth should be replaced and the cause (which may be damp getting in through a defective roof tile) removed.

Once the joists are cleaned up and any dust and loose debris removed, tongued and grooved 18mm. chipboard can be laid and screwed to the joists. Although this is more expensive than $\frac{1}{8}$in. hardboard the latter requires to be laid on battens at 9in. centres to give a sound walk-on floor. Where joints are made without the support of joists pieces of 3in. × 2in. timber should be fixed to the joists.

You may find that once the floor has been laid and it is easier to move about, it will be possible to enclose an area with boards or partitioning of a light construction.

Much can be done to make the loft warmer by the use of Marleycel expanded polystyrene of Grade 1 self-extinguishing material. This is available in standard thicknesses from $\frac{1}{2}$in. to 2in., but $\frac{1}{2}$in. thickness is recommended to be fixed with adhesive to run from purlin to purlin. Additional support can be given by triangular fillets of timber nailed to the purlins. Sheet sizes of the Marleycel are 4 × 2, 4 × 4, 6 × 2, 6 × 4, 8 × 2 and 8 × 4ft.

Two examples of the use of Marleycel Expanded Polystyrene — one as a wall veneer to cut down condensation by keeping the wall warmer and the other in its thicker form as an excellent coldwater storage tank cover.

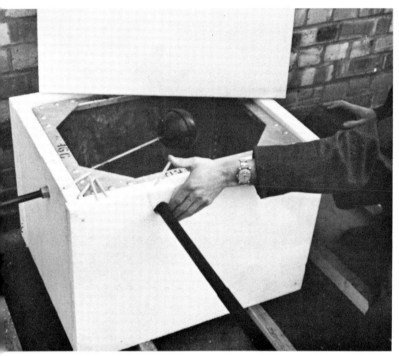

The board may be fixed direct to the rafters with the long side parallel to the eaves and joins made over a rafter. Counterbattens of $1\frac{1}{2}$ x $\frac{3}{4}$ in. should be laid over the boards and nailed through to the rafters. With $\frac{1}{2}$ in. boards the nails should be not less than $2\frac{1}{2}$ in.

Incidentally these boards make an excellent lining to walls when they are fixed direct to brick, concrete or stonework with a special adhesive applied with a serrated trowel spread over the back of the board.

If damp patches are seen on the walls of the loft or on any of the woodwork you must suspect movement or damage to the roof tiles. Sometimes small gaps of daylight can be seen indicating that the felt has perished or tiles have slipped. Pre-World War I machine-made clay tiles had a nasty habit of developing these faults and something should be done to replace them. But that is outside the scope of this book and advice should be obtained from your local Marley Tile Depot.

Some form of heating and lighting will nearly always be required even for the short periods the loft is in use and a light switch should be installed immediately inside the trap entry so that it can be operated from the top of the loft ladder.

Most pre-war houses have their electric supply cables in steel conduit and, unless you know exactly what you are doing, no attempt should be made to take in a loop for your lighting and switch gear. Get a competent electrician to do it for you.

But if you have some knowledge you will find all you need to know about fitting lighting points and switches in the 96 page booklet *Re-wiring a House* by Geoffrey Arnold. The information given conforms to the requirements of the IEE wiring regulations 14th edition. It costs 50p post paid from Burdett Workshops, 137 Torbay Road, Harrow, Middlesex, HA2 9QG.

There is only one safe form of loft heating and that is by a non-radiant black heater or oil-filled radiator with thermostat control. This should be wired up so that an indicator light on the control switch is clearly visible from outside the loft.

(8) Extending the home

If you have an urgent need for more living space and consider that the provision of an extra room in the loft involves too much interior reconstruction and too high a cost you would be very wise to consider the obvious merits of extending the home outwards. There are very few properties which do not provide a suitable area to take a standard home extension while, even in positions where the construction of the house would seem to present difficulties, some arrangement for more space can be worked out.

Given that premise how do you make a start?

Before the Building Regulations were drawn up in 1965 anyone was free to put up any old type of lean-to, garage or conservatory, and this resulted in many areas becoming—as one planning authority put it—shanty towns. In some cases it is true these erections became a certain hazard and fire risk to adjacent property. So you must look upon the restrictions now imposed by Planning Departments and the current Building Regulations as being essential to maintain the value of your own property and that of your neighbours.

However, in spite of the care with which the regulations were drawn up, there is still some confusion in the interpretation of what constitutes an extension by some local councils simply because of the uses to which the extension is put. But they are usually very helpful.

For instance although Building Regulations apply to its construction, permission is not normally refused for a small extension which does not exceed one tenth of the cubic volume of your present property or 1,750cu. ft. whichever is the greater. But approval must still be obtained.

If the proposed extension is to be used as a habitable room, a living room, bedroom, kitchen or laundry room, playroom, etc., these count as major structural alterations for which the council must give approval and they will insist that the Building Regulations are implicitly followed.

In this case scale drawings must be submitted and these should show clearly the outline of your property, the proposed site of the extension, site boundaries, the aspect, i.e. the North point, the distance from other properties, location and width of roads, etc. These are all shown on the deeds of your property as it was originally built.

If you feel that such a task is beyond your ability there's no need to give up hope for Marley Buildings Ltd. have a complete service which includes the drawing up of the necessary plans,

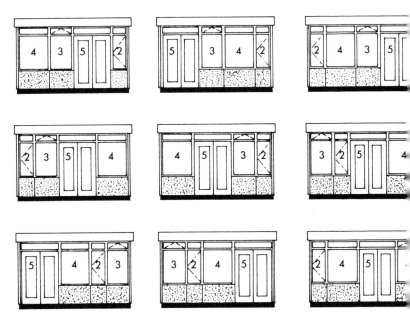

obtaining permission from the local council and supplying the whole thing for self-assembly for cash or deferred payments. They will even do the whole erection job and leave only the decoration side to you.

They have now had a vast experience of local requirements and can talk with authority to the local officials whereas an individual may feel frustrated by what he may consider to be 'red tape'.

There are a few other points to remember. An extension planned for use as a living room or bedroom must be of a high standard equal to that required in a house or bungalow. If it is to be built within 1m. (3ft. 3$\frac{5}{8}$in.) of the boundary (and this is usually the case with semi-detached or terraced property) the wall of the extension adjacent to the boundary must be of approved fire-resistant material.

This is a point to consider in personal relationships with your neighbour for he may not like the idea of a dull brick wall right next to his windows. He may object, but any claim would not be satisfied as only in very special circumstances will a court declare that he has been deprived of his rights to light. Even in the most difficult cases there is an answer—have the home extension entirely freestanding away from the boundary as a

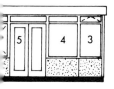

The Marley system is extremely versatile. This series of diagrams shows the alternatives possible of the 15ft. front elevation. Twelve different combinations for this front wall can be constructed to suit individual requirements.

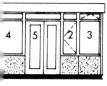

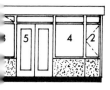

garden room. No company has done more to uplift the image of Sun Lounges and Home Extensions than Marley Buildings Ltd. At every stage in the development of their models their architects have taken cognizance of the latest Building Regulations and relevant Codes of Practice to ensure that they reach the high standards required.

With each order for a building they supply elevation and specification plans for submission to the Local Authority. A scaled sheet is provided for you to prepare a Building Plan showing the position of the proposed extension in relation to your house and the existing boundaries. As explained earlier you will be required to submit a Location Plan and this can be traced off the Local Ordnance Survey Map at your council offices. You then get Application Forms from them which you will have to complete to accompany the plans. This form requires you to state the materials used and the type of construction. All these details are given in the specification or in the drawings supplied.

The merits of the Marley Sun Lounges and Extensions are these:

1. All models are available in two different heights called 'S' and 'H', 7ft. 6in. and 8ft. 6in. overall. The clear internal heights at the rear, under the wallplate, are 7ft. 1in. and 8ft. 1in. with the roof sloping upwards to the wall. As a free-standing room the roof can slope either way as required.

2. The components in any wall are interchangeable so that doors and windows can be positioned to your exact requirements. The walls are of reinforced concrete with a choice of maintenance-free Whitespar or Marleybrick (a simulated brick finish) and are supplied with internal lining panels.

3. The large picture windows are framed in Western Red Cedar, the full size side-hung opening windows giving a low sill level and unobstructed view.

4. There are two types of roof construction, box profile translucent Marleyglaze or traditional felt and boarded construction complete with ceiling and glass-fibre insulation. A refinement which is available as an optional extra is a two layer roof of Marleyglaze which combats condensation. The depth of the roof is only $3\frac{1}{2}$ in. which means the Sun Lounge can be built on to most bungalows.

5. The preformed box gutter is concealed behind the contemporary fascia and is complete with vinyl downpipes.

6. A wiring duct for electricity supply is provided behind standard skirting boards of attractive Parana Pine.

This is a very brief picture in words, the solid construction and its versatility can be appreciated by the exploded drawing of a basic design.

Selection of a suitable model is fairly simple. You take the measurements of the internal and external length you prefer and mark these on your wall plan or wall. There should be a vertical strip of house wall 6in. wide at each end against which to fit the side walls of the sun lounge. The height should be decided by measuring to the top of the highest window or door from your proposed base level. If this height is below 7ft. 1in. you can fit the 'S' type, but if not you will have to raise the base level or choose the higher 'H' type. Also you must check

The component parts of a Marley Sun
Lounge showing how the basic design can be
adapted to a wide variety of sizes and
constructions.

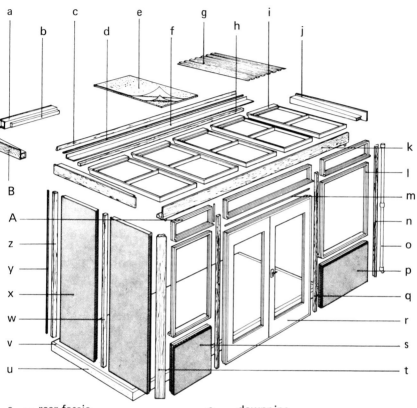

a — rear fascia
   (free-standing models only)
b — wallplate
c — timber batten
d — ½" x ½" foam strip
e — felt and boarded roof
f — flashing
g — Marleyglaze roof
h — wallplate
i — roofgrid
j — side fascia
k — front fascia
l — window frame
m — window strip
n — corner post

o — downpipe
p — cill height wall panel
q — interpost
r — double door
s — cill height wall panel
t — corner post
u — concrete base
v — damp proof course
w — interpost
x — full height wall panel
y — ½" x ½" foam strip
z — wall post
A — fanlight (type 'H' models)
B — side fascia

that the overall height of either model (7ft. 6in. or 8ft. 6in.) will fit below any projections on the house wall. Drawings are available showing how to overcome projecting chimney breasts or downpipes. It must be kept in mind that when the end wall of the extension is within 1m. (3ft. $3\frac{5}{8}$ in.) of your boundary this end must be constructed of full height wall panels to provide the required fire resistance of the Building Regulations.

Another essential point is that if the extension is to be used as a habitable room the traditional solid roof construction must be used and type 'H' model must be chosen to give the minimum ceiling height of 7ft. 6in.

These sun lounges are available in these sizes: from 9ft. in modules of 2ft. up to 29ft. long and in four widths 4ft. 6in., 6ft. 6in., 8ft. 6in. and 10ft. 6in. Two standard heights type 'S' 7ft. 6in. and 'H' 8ft. 6in.

Additional accessories are available in the form of a felt and boarded roof, wall insulation, suspended floor and venetian blinds.

While all the Sun Lounges and Home Extensions are supplied on a self-assembly basis you are expected to provide a smooth and level concrete slab for a solid floor construction or oversite concrete for a suspended timber floor.

The wall panels are cast from high density concrete and are heavy and while one normally fit person can handle the sill height panels additional help will be required when handling the full height ones.

For a competent handyman a completely self-built home extension is well within his capacity and provided he conforms to the requirements of Planning Permission and abides by the Building Regulations he can be well satisfied with his invest-ment.

Nothing improves the property more in appearance and value than the extra space provided by a Sun Lounge. These typical examples of Marley constructions are adequate proof of their investment value.

9

Improving the exterior

Every year the snow and frost of winter leave their marks on the exterior fabric of your house. Some are readily apparent, cracked downpipes and damp-stained walls, unsafe gutters, flaking brickwork and lost pointing. The front and rear elevations are crying out for a face-lift and you know that to keep up the value of your property you've either got to do the work yourself or be prepared to face a bill of £200 or more.

You know very well that a house which looks cared for will, no matter its size, command a price at least £500 more than its neglected counterpart. So it's really a matter of saying to yourself: 'Here's the simplest way I know of saving a great deal of money.'

For a satisfactory, long-lasting face-lift to the exterior of your house you need to consider these three main points:

1 Have you got, or can you borrow or hire, the right equipment to permit you to get close to the work you want to do and have you the physical capacity for what is—make no mistake about it—a fairly strenuous job?

2 All structural and repair work must be done before any decorative aspect is considered so you must phase your work plan to allow for the vagaries of the weather. It's not a good idea to remove defective gutters when a spell of wet weather is forecast!

3 You must ensure that your requirements for materials are carefully estimated—even erring on the generous side. It is very frustrating to find that you've got to make another trip to your retailer in order to finish the job. Count any little left-overs as time-savers, not as waste.

As one of the important tasks you will face is the repair or replacement of rust-corroded gutters and brackets you must appreciate that it is not an easy task if the only equipment you have is an extending ladder. It can be very arduous removing a heavy length of old iron with only one hand. A tower platform,

Installing a Marley Rainwater Gutter.
The Swanneck is made up of separate
parts and solvent welded to make
a permanent fitting.

which gives complete freedom while working at heights provides the safe way to do all the exterior work. It enables you to work with both hands free and saves the tiring effort of constantly climbing up and down. Because it allows you to be near your work it will be so much more 'professional'.

If you have a large detached property to maintain where an estimate for exterior decoration might be as high as £500 or more you may well consider that £50-60 spent on a tower platform is money well spent for you save its cost with the first major job you do. As it is dismantled into small parts it makes little demand on storage space.

For a complete exterior decoration and repair job one must be able to work at heights in complete safety. A tower platform will give you confidence and enable you to work in comfort.

Have you ever considered the importance of your gutters and downpipes and only become concerned during exceptional weather conditions which may include a cloudburst? Are they adequate to meet the worst conditions?

The technically minded might care to note these figures: The 4in. (100mm.) nominal half round gutter fitted level has a flow capacity of 8.8 gal. (40 litres) a minute, will drain a roof area of 338sq. ft. (31m.^{2}) with a pipe size of $2\frac{1}{2}$in. and outlet at one end. With an outlet in the centre the flow capacity is 17.6 gal. (80 litres) and an area of 678sq. ft. (63m.^{2}) can be drained. If set to a fall of 1in. in 50ft. (25mm. in 15.2m.) the figures are flow 12.32 gal. (56 litres) area 475sq. ft. (44m.^{2}) for a 4in. gutter with end outlet and 24.64 gal. (112 litres) flow and an area of 950sq. ft. (88m.^{2}) for a gutter with an outlet in the centre.

These figures should always be considered when replacing existing gutters or when additions to the home resulting in increased roof area are made.

Your present house will probably have gutters of cast iron. When new they are very sound as you have probably noticed when leaning a ladder against them. But without regular maintenance they deteriorate quite rapidly. It is not enough to paint only the outside.

They should be cleaned out regularly every two years for it is quite astonishing to see how much debris and soot they collect, particularly in industrial areas.

Having cleared all the debris, use a wire brush (wear goggles for this job!) to remove any rust or corrosion and give the interior a good thick coat of bituminous paint. Check also that the brackets are sound.

You may find that at the joins the gutter bolts have decayed setting up leaks and they should be replaced or the cracks made good with a waterproof mastic. A stubborn corroded bolt may be eased with a little penetrating oil or heated with a blowtorch but this is a tricky job if you have only a ladder to stand on and you must be careful not to damage the woodwork supporting the brackets. If your gutters have reached a really corroded state and you think they can be patched up, forget it. You will only have to do it again later on.

Far better to decide on a complete re-guttering job using the modern rainwater goods. They are strong, light, surprisingly easy to fix and for normal house and bungalow use are made in two sizes and two grades: 4in. (100mm.) with $2\frac{1}{2}$in. (68mm.) pipe

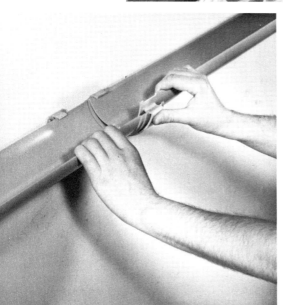

and Deepflow with 2½ in. (68mm.) pipe. They can be obtained in black, grey and white shades. Four inch (100mm.) gutter and 2½ in. (68mm.) pipe is available in two grades: Heavy and System 2 which is available in grey only. A complete range of fittings (illustrated here) enables any size, shape or style of system to be installed.

Installation instructions are these, easily followed by looking at the illustrations:

1 *Heavy grade.* Two lengths of gutter are joined by means of a gutter strap which is placed around the socket end of one

98

gutter, and the spigot end of the next length is clipped into place (Fig. 1). The gutter strap compresses the spigot against the synthetic rubber gasket making a watertight seal.

System 2. Two lengths of gutter are joined by means of a union clip which is clipped around the spigot end of one gutter, and the spigot end of the next length is snapped into place (Fig. 2). Where necessary the gutter may be cut with a fine tooth saw, and notches (Fig. 3) may be formed with a file or rasp.

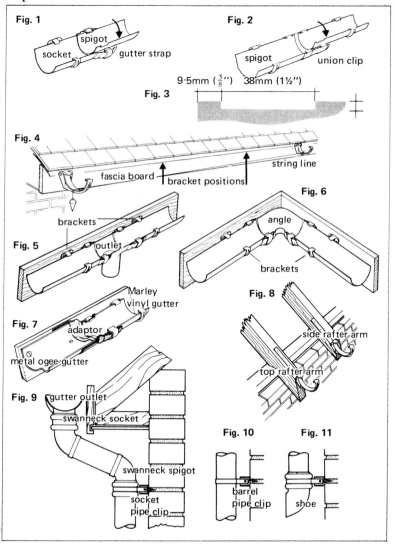

Fig. 1

socket — spigot — gutter strap

Fig. 2

spigot — union clip

9·5mm ($\frac{3}{8}$") 38mm (1½")

Fig. 3

Fig. 4

fascia board — bracket positions — string line

brackets

Fig. 5

outlet

Fig. 6

angle

brackets

Fig. 7

Marley vinyl gutter

adaptor

metal ogee gutter

Fig. 8

side rafter arm

top rafter arm

Fig. 9

gutter outlet

swanneck socket

swanneck spigot

socket pipe clip

Fig. 10

barrel pipe clip

Fig. 11

shoe

2 *Bracket fixing.* The brackets are fixed at a maximum of 0.914m. (3ft. 0in.) centres on the fascia board. To obtain the correct fall, use a string line and mark the bracket positions accordingly (Fig. 4). The spacing should also be arranged so that each gutter joint has a close supporting bracket, or brackets in the case of a union clip joint. Angles and outlets should have close supporting brackets also (Figs 5 and 6). Top and side rafter arms are available for brackets (Fig. 8). Old terraced houses with metal ogee gutters require the cast aluminium ogee H.R. vinyl adaptor designed for connecting Marley vinyl gutter to metal ogee gutter (Fig. 7).

3 *Pipe joints.* The rainwater pipe is usually fixed externally and the joint between the spigot and socket left unsealed.

4 *Swanneck fixing.* The socket of the swanneck is engaged on the spigot of the gutter outlet, and the socket of the first length of pipe engages on the spigot of the swanneck. The swanneck spigots are supplied long enough to be trimmed to the correct length for the first socket pipe clip to be fixed into a mortar joint (Fig. 9).

5 *Pipe clip fixing.* A socket pipe clip is located between the two ribs on pipe or fitting sockets. An intermediate barrel clip should be provided in the centre of every pipe length of 2m. (6ft. 7in.) (Fig. 10).

6 *Shoe fixing/drain connection.* The pipe may terminate with a shoe (Fig. 11), or alternatively can be connected directly to the underground drain with a cement mortar joint, incorporating a special disc drain adaptor.

For the discriminating householder, faced with a renewal of his rainwater system, who will go to extra trouble to give his house a new look there are other Marley systems well worth consideration which have been highly praised by architects and builders. These are the Anglia—a rectilinear gutter with rectangular pipe; the Classic with a distinctive ogee profile and the recently introduced Deepflow and Deepflow Box Eaves.

The smaller size of rainwater goods, with 3in. wide gutters and 2in. pipes is also a complete system in itself and is used for garages, extensions, sheds, lean-tos, etc., where it is perfectly adequate in coping with the heaviest downpour. (See page 143).

The end can terminate in a water butt or storage tank if you need the rainwater but it may be advisable in many cases to fit an overflow to the nearest gulley or soakaway.

A twentieth century version in plastic of the Ogee gutter, showing the profile of the 'Classic' gutter and downpipe as fixed on a brick-built modern home.

The new Marley Anglia gutter in a modern rectilinear profile.

The illustrations show the complete range of fittings available and the instructions which are simple enough for anyone to follow (see page 144).

A. Clip gutter into the socket under the retaining nibs to complete joint. Whenever a 2m. (6ft. 7in.) length of gutter is cut, notches must be filed on the gutter ends to the same dimensions as those supplied with the full 2m. (6ft. 7in.) lengths.

B. Vinyl gutter bracket (RK 301) screwed into position on fascia. Method of introducing 3in. (75mm.) gutter in brackets in order to ensure that the gutter is held securely.

C. Note position of fascia brackets near to each side of the union clip (RU 30).

Bracket spacings must not exceed 3ft. centres.

Join gutter lengths together by using a union clip (RU 30) as shown.

D. This installation can be assembled at ground level, bracket positions marked on fascia and spacings *must not exceed 3ft. centres.* Gutters then lifted and turned into position as in B.

E. If it is not possible to fix brackets to the framework on a greenhouse then a 2in. (51mm.) x $\frac{1}{2}$in. (12.7mm.) fascia should be fixed across the glazing bars.

Having satisfied yourself that your gutters and downpipes are sound, that any gullies or soakaways are not blocked, attention can now be given to any obvious faults in the exterior finish.

Patches of pebbledash, or Tyrolean finish, or rendering may have remained discoloured after heavy rain whereas the rest of the area has dried out. Here you must suspect that these areas have come away from the brickwork and that sooner or later they will fall away in chunks.

You can test this by lightly tapping the wall and if it sounds hollow you should ring round the areas with coloured chalk for they must be removed and the gaps made good.

Knock away all the loose material with a bolster chisel and hammer but do it carefully to keep the area to be replaced to a minimum. For this work one of the four Marleymixes is ideal. This should be the Bricklaying Mortar and Rendering Mix which is easily identified by its mauve tape closure. A large bag contains 0.93cu. ft. which will cover an area of 35sq. ft. (3.30m.^{2}) rendered $\frac{3}{8}$in. (10mm.) thick. The bag should be

GUTTER AND FITTINGS		100mm (4") size
	Heavy Grade Gutter	length 2m (6' 7")
	System 2 Gutter grey only	3m (9' 10")
	Gutter Angle	90° 120° 135°
	Outlet 2 Sockets	drop size 65mm (2½")
	Stopend Outlet	drop size 65mm (2½")
	Union Clip	
	Stopend Internal	
	Stopend External	
	Gutter Strap	
	Fascia Bracket	
	Side Rafter Arm inc. 2 nuts and bolts	
	Top Rafter Arm inc. 2 nuts and bolts	
	Rise & Fall Extension Arm	
	Angled Fascia Bracket Adaptor	22½° 30°

	Ogee/H.R. Vinyl Gutter Adaptor	left hand right hand
	Gutter Notching Tool	bench tool

PIPE AND FITTINGS		65mm (2½") size
	Heavy Grade Pipe	length 2m (6' 7") 2·5m (8' 2½") 3m (9' 10")
	System 2 Pipe	2m (6' 7") 2·5m (8' 2½") 3m (9' 10")
	Branch	92½° 112½° 135°
	Swanneck	projection 152mm (6") 229mm (9") 305mm (12")
	Hopper Head	
	Loose Pipe Socket	

	Bend	92½° 112½° 135°
	Swanneck End Socket	
	Swanneck End Spigot	
	Swanneck Bend	
	Shoe	
	Disc Drain Adaptor	
	Pipe Clip	socket barrel
	One Piece Pipe Clip	barrel
	Extension Pipe Bracket	socket barrel
	Drive-in Pipe Bracket	socket barrel
	Solvent Cement	

shaken up before use and the correct amount of water added to give a fairly dry mix. First 7 pints (4 litres) of water should be added and well mixed and then another pint (0.5 litres) added. The added plasticiser in the mix makes it easy to work and its moderate strength resists cracking in extremes of temperature.

Some areas of faulty pebbledash may be of an inch or more in thickness and the new rendering should be applied in several coats allowing each one to dry before the levelling coat is applied. The washed aggregate (pebbles) should be thrown from a shovel at the final damp area and very lightly pressed into the mix with a float.

Wide cracks in rendering can be filled with the same mix but you may find it easy to fill fine cracks with a waterproof filler. One of the ways to cut down the work of exterior decoration—and one which is becoming increasingly popular—is to cover large areas of dull brickwork with rigid PVC cladding. This is a very practical proposition as its advantages are that it will not suffer from corrosion, erosion, frost or damp. Once fitted, it requires no maintenance and can be kept in its bright white condition simply by washing it over with a mild detergent when necessary.

In some areas where local councils may consider it alters the character of the house it may be necessary to get Planning Permission.

Marley vinyl claddings are available in five profiles: Shiplap, Tradlap, Weatherboard (like traditional wooden boarding), M-Lap and V-Lap. Each may be used horizontally or vertically, though the first three were intended for horizontal use and the two latter for vertical use.

Sizes are these: Shiplap 4m. and 5m. long, cover width 100mm. Tradlap 4m. and 5m. long, cover width 135mm. Weatherboard 4m. and 5m., cover width 150mm. M-Lap and V-Lap are in 3m. lengths covering 150mm.

Method of fixing which is clearly described in a six page folder is by way of vertical timber battens of $1\frac{3}{4} \times \frac{3}{4}$ in. softwood at a maximum distance of 16in. centres, or to any groundwork which will take and hold a clout nail. Aluminium fixing cleats (one is supplied with each foot of cladding ordered) are fixed to the battens with aluminium clout nails and the first plank is hooked into the line of cleats and so on.

The result is a firmly fixed permanent facing which will greatly enhance the appearance and value of your house.

Traditional methods of exterior decoration will always appeal

VINYL CLADDING
Component details and dimensions

General
Marley Rigid PVC Claddings are readily fixed to new or old buildings. They are impermeable to water, tough, durable and need no maintenance, retaining their smart appearance unmarred by dents or peeling surfaces.

There are five profiles available: Tradlap, Shiplap and Weatherboard, primarily designed for horizontal applications although they can equally well be used vertically; M-Lap and V-Lap primarily designed for vertical applications, although these may be used equally well horizontally.

The claddings consist of lengths of interlocking planks with cover widths as follows:

Profile	Stock Lengths	Cover Width
Tradlap	4m and 5m	135mm (5¼")
Standard Shiplap	4m and 5m	100mm (4")
Weatherboard	4m and 5m	150mm (6")
M-Lap	3m	150mm (6")
V-Lap	3m	150mm (6")

(1 cleat supplied per foot).

Material
Marley Vinyl Claddings are manufactured from rigid PVC a material well-known in the Building Industry for its toughness, resilience and good external weathering qualities. It will not suffer from corrosion, erosion, frost or damp.

Colour
White — Suitable for external and internal use. Some profiles are available in Stone and Burgundy.

Thermal Movement
Rigid PVC moves approximately 6·4mm (¼") for every 1·83m (6') of length over a temperature change of 38° C (100° F). If for example a 4m plank is fixed on a colder day when its temperature is 0°C (32F) and later it becomes heated by the sun in high summer to 56°C (132° F) it will expand 12·7mm (½"). These extreme conditions at the time of fixing would be unusual in the U.K. but the design and methods of fixing Marley Vinyl Claddings allow for them.

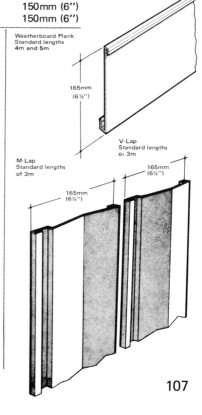

Shiplap Plank
Standard lengths
4m and 5m

115mm (4½")

76mm (3")

Tradlap
Standard lengths
4m and 5m

150mm (6")

104mm (4⅛")

Weatherboard Plank
Standard lengths
4m and 5m

165mm (6½")

V-Lap
Standard lengths
or 3m

165mm (6½")

M-Lap
Standard lengths
of 3m

165mm (6½")

107

Replacement Plank

115mm
(4½")

Rigid PVC Channel
Standard length
3·05m (10')

50mm (2")

16mm
(⅔")

Aluminum Fixing
Cleat

40mm
(1⅝")

28mm
(1⅛")

External Angle
Standard length 3·05m(10')

Internal Angle
Standard length
3·05m (10")

19mm
(¾")

19mm
(¾")

50mm
(2")

35mm (1⅝")

Batten
38 x 19mm

28mm

New Starter Strip
with rear flange

19mm

New Top Finishing Piece

14mm

28mm

Batten
38 x 19mm

'Z' Section
With or without
rear flange (a)

50mm
(2")

a

108

FIXING (Horizontal)

Batten out with 38mm x 19mm
(1½" x ¾") vertical softwood battens
at a maximum of 406mm (16") centres.
Fig. 1. A double batten should be fixed
wherever a channel is used at abutments
or corners. Alternatively, cladding may
be fixed direct to studding at no more
than 406mm (16") centres or to any
groundwork which will take and hold a
clout nail. Care should be taken to line
up the face of the groundwork in order
to provide a true level finish. The
finished result will only be as good as the
groundwork to which the cladding is
fixed.

Fix channel down each side of panel,
down the sides of openings such as
doors, windows and along the top under
soffits and under window sills **Fig. 7.**
When cladding more than one wall and
using internal or external angles, slip the
two channels into the cover piece and
fix the channels on each side of the
corner. Nails should be driven firmly but
not tightly home, so that the channel is
free to expand or contract. A 6mm (¼")
gap is left between the top of the
channel and the head of the panel. This
allows the channel to move upwards with
changes in temperature. The channel
should be bedded in mastic or
alternatively some other precaution taken
to prevent water penetration between
the cladding and adjacent materials when
fixed against an abutment.

Fix a straight line of cleats **Fig. 3** or
fix starter strip **Fig. 4** at the foot of the
panel with aluminium clout nails. The
ends of the starter strip are entered
12mm (½") into the channel at each
side **Fig. 5.** Always so position the first
plank or starter strip so that it allows a
minimum drip of 6mm (¼") at the foot
of panel **Fig. 4.**

The first plank is hooked into the
line of cleats or the starter strip, and
entered half way into the channel on
each side and nail fixed at the centre.
See **Fig. 3.** Planks can be pulled firmly
into each lock or unlocked a maximum
of 5mm ($\frac{3}{16}$") on each lock to give
flexibility in cover width.

The last full-width plank which will
fit is finished within 100mm (4") of the

top of the panel. A new plank is then selected and the appropriate amount sawn from the top of the plank.

A thin ribbon or strip of solvent-weld adhesive is then run along the rear of the top sawn edge. The plank is then offered up and pushed home between the 'J' hooks inside the top finishing piece **Fig. 6.**

This system of finishing means that the fixing has been reduced to the minimum with consequent savings in time and labour.

Providing provision is made for the planks to move and the ends and sides to be weathered, there is no objection to the use of other materials instead of the channel. For instance a wooden window frame is sometimes rebated to take the plank and in a flat roof fascia the top trim may be used in lieu of channel. However in these cases it is important that the trim is at least 28mm ($1\frac{1}{8}''$) deep. If so desired the head of a panel can be weathered with traditional metal flashings.

The top finishing piece is designed to finish the top of a panel so that it is unnecessary to use a flashing.

Channel is used to weather gable ends, doors, windows and other openings **Fig. 7 & 8.**

Fig 1
Timber Battens
(Horizontal Cladding)

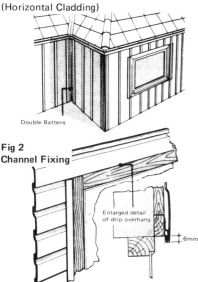

Double Battens

Fig 2
Channel Fixing

Enlarged detail of drip overhang

6mm

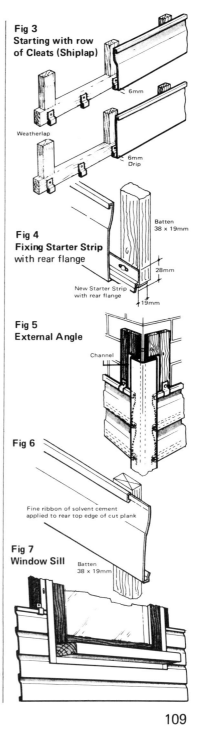

Fig 3
Starting with row of Cleats (Shiplap)

6mm

Weatherlap

6mm Drip

Batten 38 x 19mm

Fig 4
Fixing Starter Strip with rear flange

28mm

New Starter Strip with rear flange

19mm

Fig 5
External Angle

Channel

Fig 6

Fine ribbon of solvent cement applied to rear top edge of cut plank

Fig 7
Window Sill

Batten 38 x 19mm

**Fig 8
Gable End**

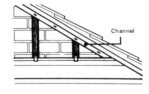

Channel

**Fig 9
Lap Joint**

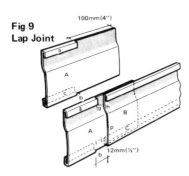

100mm (4")

A
B

12mm (½")

**Fig 10
Butt Joint**

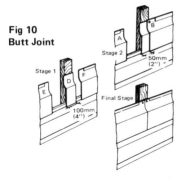

Stage 2
Stage 1
50mm (2")
Final Stage
100mm (4")

**Fig 11
Vertical Fixing**

Side Channel

Z-Section

Replacement Plank (Patent applied for)
When a plank has been damaged by an external force, it can be easily repaired using the replacement plank. First remove the damaged planks. Replace all except the last plank with good material fixed in the normal way. Adjust the locking bar in position and nail. Finally position the replacement plank and engage by exerting pressure on the outside of the plank **Fig. 12.**

**Fig 12
Replacement Plank**

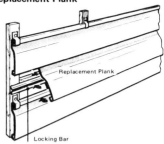

Replacement Plank

Locking Bar

Ground work
Marley Claddings may be fixed direct to fair faced building blocks provided they will take and hold clout head nails. They may also be fixed to studding or other timber grounds providing the cleats are not more than 406mm (16") apart.

Cleaning
On completing fixing the Cladding, and when work around it is finished, it should be washed clean with a weak solution of detergent.

Handling and Storage
Marley Claddings may be drilled with a standard twist drill and sawn with a fine tooth saw. They must always be fixed with cleats or through slotted holes. Never cut planks tightly between abutments. Never nail directly through sheet. When stored, planks should be laid flat and covered to avoid damage.

Uses
As external and internal cladding to: domestic houses, office blocks and industrial buildings. As decorative finishes in: exhibitions, shop fittings, furniture, counters, fences, partitions, balconies, lightweight doors, screens and window boxes. Suitable for vertical and horizontal applications.

110

Vinyl cladding can enhance
the appearance of the exterior
and is particularly suitable
for porches.

to the amateur and for those who must consider the cost factor cement based paints will be chosen. Many home decorators who have mastered the necessary techniques which include the thorough brushing of the old surface, sealing any powdery surfaces with the right primer, not mixing too much paint at one time, etc., do a first class job, but the careless amateur can get himself into a horrible mess and the cleaning up can be a formidable task.

Unless you are prepared to follow the instructions very carefully it might be better to use one of the special finishes produced for the amateur. These comparatively new formulations with vinyl and special additives for adhesion, retention of colour and resistance to the weather would probably prove better in the long run.

Many home decorators make the mistake in thinking that painting exterior woodwork and metal is for decorative purposes only whereas its most important function is protective. It is no good giving these areas another lick of paint on a surface which is already broken down.

All metalwork showing the effects of corrosion should be cleaned to bright metal, given the correct primer followed by a good quality undercoat and the best quality gloss paint. If a thixotropic (jelly) paint is chosen make sure you do not brush it out too much, especially on sharp edges and corners. But remember that too thick a coating on metal window frames may result in difficulty in closing them.

It is important to see that timber to be repainted must be in sound condition. Danger areas are window sills and framework. Where there are big blisters you may find rotting wood underneath and of course this must be cut away to sound wood and replaced. A waterproof filler can be applied to cracks or to open grain woodwork and when dry primed and undercoated. Two undercoats and one finishing coat should give the necessary protection.

Finally before you stand back to admire your efforts take a look at the air bricks which ventilate any suspended timber floors. Push a thin cane into the holes to make sure there is no obstruction and certainly clear away any soil which have accidentally covered the air bricks.

And while you are doing this take a look at the damp course to ensure that this has not been bridged or damaged.

10
Housing the car

One of the easiest, and most common, ways of throwing away hard-earned money is to buy an expensive new car and condemn it to early depreciation by leaving it out in all weathers.

If you have no space to erect a garage or carport you are, of course, always on the losing end, for if you value your car and want to house it you may face a weekly rental of £1.00 or more if you can find a place under cover for it!

Look down any street in any suburb and you will find thousands of semi-detached homes with space for a car under cover where the cars are parked in the road or pulled into front gardens where they are at the mercy of the elements. In both cases they cause congestion or annoyance.

Car owners who put up with this need to have their heads examined for the simplest arithmetic shows that if a car depreciates by £200 a year this is more than the cost of a well-built, average size garage which, apart from saving you money, will certainly add several hundred pounds to the value of your property if you come to sell it.

In fact property without a garage or carport will always be more difficult to sell than one with housing for the car. And it is also true that more and more homeseekers are seeking property offering accommodation for *two* cars now that Britain is rapidly becoming a two-car owning family nation.

Certainly if you have the space you should get yourself a double garage, or a garage and a carport, and you should ask yourself these questions before you decide to invest in one, or to replace the decrepit one left to you by the previous owner of the property.

Will you want to store other items in it? Do you want space and a workbench for hobbies and car maintenance? Will the number of cars in the family increase? Is the type of car you have likely to change and perhaps be larger?

You must also bear in mind that although the erection of a

garage is called 'Permitted Development' it may mean that you have to have modifications to a pavement (installing a drop curb for example) while if your proposal means the making of a new 'vehicular access to a trunk or classified road' Planning Permission will have to be obtained. Some councils insist in this case that a turning circle is made on the owner's property so that cars do not reverse on to this class of road.

Do you know, for example, what the dimensions of your present car are? A Mini is just over 10ft. long by 4ft. $7\frac{1}{2}$in. wide. Fords run from 13ft. to 15ft. 6in. or so, whereas a Jaguar will require something bigger than a standard 16ft. long garage. Quite obviously car length and width must be the major factor in choosing.

Marley claim to be the largest company in the world manufacturing and erecting concrete garages and buildings. Certainly they have a fantastic range of designs and different models at competitive prices, which enable you to choose a garage to harmonise with your surroundings. You also have a choice of erecting the garage yourself or you can employ one of their fully-equipped erection teams, specially trained to do an efficient and speedy job. And where Planning Permission is necessary, or Building Regulations make a certain specification necessary, expert advice and assistance are provided.

Normally, most Marley garages can be erected over a week-end with the assistance of another person. You have to provide a base and this must be a few inches larger in length and width than the garage itself. Usually a 4in. thickness of concrete on a 6in. bed of consolidated hardness is adequate as a foundation.

The Sparlite wall finish comprising selected natural stone particles is applied during construction of the panels, needs no maintenance and is permanent. However it can be colour washed or emulsion painted to blend with the finish on adjacent properties, if this is preferred.

General specification includes reinforcement of the panels with steel to the requirements of British Standard No. 785 or 1221. Walls have integral vertical tongued and grooved weather joints. Roofs on most models have grey moulded asbestos cement sheeting but there is a Tiled-Roof Garage for those who want a traditional roof. All assembly bolts, nuts and washers are rust-resistant and external bolt heads are concealed to give a clean look to exterior walls. There is a wide choice of up-and-over or side-hung doors. Fixed windows 28in. × 11in.

114

A Magnate Marley Garage can be erected by two men in a weekend.

(0.711m. × 0.279m.) are cast in wall panels for glazing direct to the concrete surround but additional larger timber framed windows (fixed or opening) can be obtained as optional extras. Rainwater gutters of the Marley PVC type can be supplied complete for little additional cost.

For those only interested in economy there is the Master Model with redwood side-hung doors and four fixed windows. Optional accessories include a personal door in either flank, guttering to rear wall, additional fixed or opening windows, shelf brackets and even a collapsible workbench/tool cabinet. The doors may be fully boarded or partly glazed. This garage is available in three sizes with internal measurements of 13ft. 4in. × 8ft., 14ft. 8in. × 8ft. and 16ft. 0in. × 8ft. Door opening sizes in each case are 7ft. 6in. wide 6ft. high. Prices range from about £103 to £113. A twin model of the Master is also available.

For a virtually maintenance-free garage there is the System Eight (R) Model with a choice of five Autodors in timber, galvasteel, aluminium and Teakcote cedar. Interior sizes are 16ft., 17ft. 4in. and 18ft. 8in. all 8ft. wide. Door opening height is 6ft. 3in. and width 7ft. 6in. Prices from about £142 to £165. A twin version of this garage is also available.

The popular Marquis, with its red cedar fascias to front and flank walls, is made in the same sizes and can have side-hung doors partly glazed in redwood or cedar or Autodors in five different

A Cedar Autodor, up and over, with the Marley Buildings' Magnate Garage.

versions. The range of prices here is from £133 to £160 or so. Twin model of this costs in the region of £228 to £280.

The Daily Mail Blue Ribbon Award winner is the Magnate with its attractive offset front panel giving an internal width of 9ft. 4in. Like certain other models this garage can be supplied with a rear annexe. Internal lengths are 16ft., 17ft. 4in. and 18ft. 8in. Side-hung doors or Autodors can be specified, according to choice.

An even bigger version of this is the Major giving an internal width of 10ft. 8in.

In the range of double garages with an aluminium up-and-over Autodor is the Monaco in three standard lengths and with an internal width of 16ft. at prices ranging from about £286 to £308.

'Brick front' garages with up-and-over doors, single or twin, lead to the handsome Meteor type with wall panels finished in Scandinavian 'Whitespar' aggregate and there is also the Marathon which offers space for two cars nose-to-tail where space for a standard double garage is not available.

Internal lengths give measurements of from 20ft. to 37ft. 4in. in increments of 1ft. 4in. Interior width is 8ft. Either side-hung or up-and-over doors can be fitted.

Height is always a problem with caravans, autovans and dormobiles, but the Merchant garage provides the answer for with three lengths of 16ft., 17ft. 4in. and 18ft. 8in. internally the door opening is 8ft. 10in. wide by 7ft. 6in. high and the internal width is 9ft. 4in. There's a twin model to this, too. However even this does not complete the selection for in the pitched roof range there is the handsome Monarch, the Merit and the superb Tiled Roof garage all available with side-hung or up-and-over doors in timber or metal. The Magna with its low-pitch roof and the Aristocratic Majestic are also included in this range. The latter is a large family size garage which will house two, three or four cars depending upon the length selected, as 16in. extensions can be added to the large 24ft. 6in. model. This size costs in the region of £300 to £400, with an aluminium up-and-over door and cost for erection by a skilled team ranging from £34 to £55, depending on the size of garage and the distance of the site from the nearest Marley Buildings factory.

Merit

Marquis

118

Majestic

Twin Brick Front

A short selection of garages from Marley Buildings Ltd.

Where a garage is not possible the next best thing is a carport and here the regulations of what kind you can have vary from one area to the next.

Here again, 'Permitted Development' allows a structure up to a capacity of 1,750cu. ft. to give cover to the car—but Building Regulations insist that the carport must be constructed of approved materials. This is sensible enough because it has been known for a car fire to be passed on to the adjacent building.

The definition between a carport and a garage is clear enough. If the structure has less than two open ends it is classified as a garage and must conform to all requirements, but a roof fixed one side to the house and made of non-combustible material supported by posts of non-combustible material will nearly always be accepted providing there is adequate space between the carport and the adjacent property.

So anyone proposing to build their own carport should use metal posts and a roofing material such as Marleyglaze, which is classified as self-extinguishing in accordance with B.S. 2782 as required in the Building Regulations.

A Marley Buildings Carport comes ready for assembly with plastic sleeved metal uprights and all the necessary fittings to make an attractive cover for the car

Marleyglaze Super Sheet is available from all retail outlets in two profiles, a box section and 3in. corrugation and three lengths 6ft. (1.83m.), 8ft. (2.44m.) and 10ft. (3.05m.) in natural translucent. The rigid PVC sheets, approx. 0.8mm. thick, are 30in. wide but the cover width, as sheets must be overlapped by one section, are 28in. (711mm.) for the box profile and $25\frac{7}{8}$in. (657mm.) for the corrugated 3in. profile.

Fixing the sheets is quite straightforward using the drive nails, washers and caps supplied in tens in each fixing pack. They must be fixed to timber purlins at no more than 30in. centres and at first and last corrugations and every third along each purlin. Holes one-eighth inch larger than the size of the screws being used must be drilled through the sheet with hand or power drill run at lowest speed. In exposed locations any structure should have additional purlins and fixings to prevent vibration in a strong wind.

Cutting the sheets should be done with a fine toothed saw with the sheet well supported. Being of rigid plastic the sheets are easier to cut in warm weather.

Foam eaves fillers are available for both profiles in 30in. widths and should be used to reduce wind passage in the corrugations. A top apron flashing for the 3in. profile, 30in. wide, is used set into the brickwork of the house wall to make an effective seal of wall to roof. In span roof construction use the 3in. ridge piece to cover the ends.

For those with more ambitious projects in mind other types of Marleyglaze should be considered. There's a Big Six sheet with a cover width of 40in. and a Standard sheet with 3in. corrugations. These are for commercial application but are obtainable for individual use.

Complete kits for the erection of carports or sunports are available from Marley Buildings Ltd. Supporting posts $1\frac{1}{2}$in. in diameter for 7ft. high models and 2in. for 7ft. to 9ft. high are of tubular steel, galvanised to resist rust and covered with white vinyl sleeves giving a complete maintenance-free finish. The roof framing also of galvanised steel, can be painted to match any colour scheme. The steel posts should be inserted 15in. below ground level and made secure by the use of the Marleymix 1 : 2 : 4 concrete.

The roof is made up of galvanised steel rafters and purlins
(cont. on p. 124)

Marleyglaze—an ideal roofing
material for car ports, covered ways
and sunlounges.

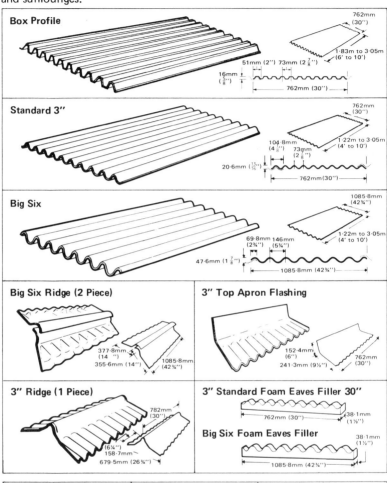

Box Profile

762mm (30")

1·83m to 3·05m (6' to 10')

51mm (2") 73mm (2 7/8")

16mm (5/8")

762mm (30")

Standard 3"

762mm (30")

1·22m to 3·05m (4' to 10')

104·8mm (4 1/8") 73mm (2 7/8")

20·6mm (13/16")

762mm (30")

Big Six

1085·8mm (42¾")

1·22m to 3·05m (4' to 10')

69·8mm (2¾") 146mm (5¾")

47·6mm (1 7/8")

1085·8mm (42¾")

Big Six Ridge (2 Piece)

377·8mm (14")

355·6mm (14")

1085·8mm (42¾")

3" Top Apron Flashing

152·4mm (6")

241·3mm (9½")

762mm (30")

3" Ridge (1 Piece)

782mm (30")

(6¼")

158·7mm

679·5mm (26¾")

3" Standard Foam Eaves Filler 30"

762mm (30")

38·1mm (1½")

Big Six Foam Eaves Filler

38·1mm (1½")

1085·8mm (42¾")

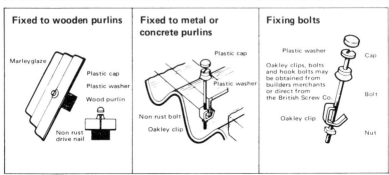

Fixed to wooden purlins

Marleyglaze

Plastic cap

Plastic washer

Wood purlin

Non rust drive nail

Fixed to metal or concrete purlins

Plastic cap

Plastic washer

Non rust bolt

Oakley clip

Fixing bolts

Plastic washer

Oakley clips, bolts and hook bolts may be obtained from builders merchants or direct from the British Screw Co.

Oakley clip

Cap

Bolt

Nut

Fixing

Standard roof fixings when used with asbestos cement sheet, e.g. Oakley clips, hook bolts, screw nails. When fixed as a complete roofing or cladding it is recommended that plastic washers and caps are used. These can be supplied with the sheet. Holes may be drilled with a hand or power tool having a Standard twist drill 3·2mm ($\frac{1}{8}$") larger in diameter than the fixing screws or bolts. It is recommended that the drill cutting angle at point be 60° to 90°. Nails must on no account be hammered through the sheet. It is not necessary to mitre the sheet as is done with asbestos.

Where the sheet is required to be cut a sheeting or pad handle hacksaw is recommended. Side lap should be 69·8mm (2¾") and end lap 152·4mm (6") on the Standard six sheet 104·8mm (4$\frac{1}{8}$") side lap and 152·4mm (6") end lap on the Standard 3" sheet, or where used in conjunction with other material should follow that used in the application. Sealing, if required, should be with approved mastic or asbestos wick.

FIXINGS

Non-rust drive screws, nails, bolts or hook bolts with matching plastic washers

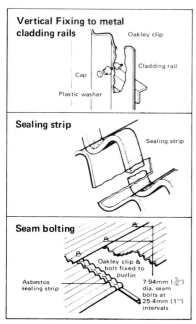

Vertical Fixing to metal cladding rails

Oakley clip

Cladding rail

Cap

Plastic washer

Sealing strip

Sealing strip

Seam bolting

Oakley clip & bolt fixed to purlin

Asbestos sealing strip

7·94mm ($\frac{5}{16}$") dia. seam bolts at 25·4mm (1") intervals

and caps should be used. Polythene packs containing matching washers and caps and drive nails can be supplied with the sheet. For use with 3" or Flat Sheet.

The minimum recommended pitch for Marleyglaze is 5°. It does not absorb water and therefore can be laid at lower pitches than asbestos and we recommend the following:

Pitch	End Laps
22½°	152·4mm (6")
15°	152·4mm (6") with end laps sealed
10°-5°	152·4mm (6") with all laps sealed

These recommendations are for normal sites. Very exposed sites and/or lower pitches may require extra precautions.

Fixing Flat Sheets

Flat Marleyglaze can be used for glazing. Waterproofing is achieved by using a mastic jointing. In areas larger than 304·8mm x 304·8mm (12" x 12") flat Marleyglaze being flexible must be firmly attached to glazing bars or frame surround to prevent it becoming bent and pushed out of position by a strong blow in the centre. It is recommended that 1·6mm ($\frac{1}{16}$") Marleyglaze be supported in panels not greater than 406·4mm (16") square.

Purlin Spacing

The maximum distance apart for the spacing of purlins should be: Big Six Profile 1371·6mm (4' 6"). All other Profiles 914·4mm (3' 0").

Bending

Big Six Profile—Is not recommended for curved surfaces. 3" Profile—Minimum bending radius of 2·43mm (8' 0").

Storing

Marleyglaze sheets should be stacked flat on clean, firm level ground. If stored in the open they should be covered with a tarpaulin or similar non-translucent sheet to avoid damage. On uneven ground timber baulks should be used.

Chemical Resistance

Marleyglaze is unaffected by dilute acids, air pollution or saline atmosphere. Can be safely installed in exposed positions on the coast as well as in areas where air pollution is excessive.

NOTE: Do not leave unfixed sheets uncovered in the open in strong sunlight.

123

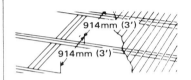

Always fix to purlins. Distance between purlins should not exceed 1372mm (4ft. 6in.) centre to centre for Big Six and 914mm (3ft.) centre to centre for other profiles.

Support both sides of sheet when cutting. Use a pad handle hacksaw.

Fixing packs containing 10 drive nails, 10 washers and 10 caps in matching colours are recommended for use with Marleyglaze except with Big Six when longer fixings are necessary.

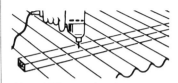

When drilling, use hand or power tool with standard twist drill. A cutting angle at point of 60° to 90° is recommended. Make holes 3.2mm ($\frac{1}{8}$″) diameter oversize. Do not hammer nails or screws through the sheet.

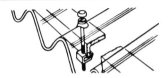

Use Oakley clips and bolts with metal or concrete purlins. Always use non-rust fixings and plastic washers and caps.

which are fitted together by stainless steel assembly bolts. A white plastic coated steel fascia for the front is also supplied. The Marleyglaze roof is fixed with hook bolts and plastic sealing washers.

The four types produced are:

1 Wall mounted model with side drainage.

2 Free-standing model with side drainage.

3 Free-standing model with end drainage.

4 Twin free-standing model with end drainage.

Lengths range from 6ft. to 30ft. 6in. in 6ft., 8ft. and 9ft. widths, for single models; and 11ft. 6in., 15ft. 6in. and 17ft. 6in. for twin versions.

⑪
Jobs around the house

When you have a concreting job to do—such as a path to lay, a drive to put down, concrete spurs for fence repair to make, crazy paving or slabs to put down—do you rush out and order a load of builders sand aggregate and bags of cement?

If you do, you'll probably have the sand piled on the pavement or drive where it can easily become contaminated or fouled and there's no fun transporting heavy bags of cement. You probably won't be able to decide exactly what type of sand is there and what its proportion to aggregate is or how much water is in the stuff. This leads to all kinds of haphazard mixings, quite unsuitable for the varied jobs for which it was originally ordered.

In these enlightened days even the beginner must be aware that there is 'the right material for the right job' and this is especially true when it comes to concrete mixtures. The introduction of ready-mixed bags of formulations of cement, sand and/or aggregate has revolutionised concreting work for amateurs and, like many innovations for do-it-yourself, has become a standard practice in much of the commercial building work done today.

If you have any sort of concreting or rendering to do it is important to know exactly what is available and the most likely source of supply for the quantities you need.

First of all the four grades of Marleymix, each of which is packed in stout multi-walled paper sacks, are these:

Fine Concrete Mix. This is for paths, the top 2in. surface of drives and crazy paving. It is a high strength mix of $\frac{3}{8}$in. down to fine-washed and graded flint aggregate, washed sharp sand and cement in a nominal 1 : 2 : 4 mix by volume. It has a plasticising agent to ensure ease of working. The coverage is about 10sq. ft. at 1in. thickness per large bag, but a medium sized bag can be obtained for small jobs.

1 : 2 : 4 Concrete Mix. This is a stronger mix for drives, concrete bases for garages, etc., and consists of $3\frac{1}{2}$ parts of $\frac{3}{4}$in.

down gravel, $2\frac{1}{2}$ parts sand and 1 part cement with a plasticising agent. The coverage is $9\frac{1}{2}$ sq. ft. at 1in. thickness per large bag. It is important to ensure that excessive water is not added to this mix.

Cement Mortar Mix. Use this one for floor surfacing, pointing between slab paving, crazy paving and for all 'making good' work. Based upon a 3 : 1 ratio of washed sharp sand and cement plus a plasticising agent it covers 11 sq. ft. at 1in. thickness per large bag. For small jobs it is available in both 'handy' and 'medium' bags.

Bricklaying Mortar & Rendering Mix. A carefully graded sand: plasticisers and cement make this suitable for bricklaying, blocklaying, internal or external rendering. When used for pointing its colour remains constant. Coverage is 35 sq. ft. at a thickness of $\frac{3}{8}$ in. per large bag or sufficient mortar to lay 66 bricks.

It should be noted that when using the ready-mixed bags containing aggregate it is advisable to turn out the contents onto a clean flat surface and give it another mixing as the aggregate can have the tendency to sink to the bottom of the bag. Return what you do not use to the bag, carefully seal it and store it in a dry place.

If you propose to put down a drive to your garage you have two alternatives, either to order a load of ready-mixed concrete or to lay a drive or paving stones or flags.

The first plan entails careful preparation of the drive area, consolidation of the ground by the use of hard core and ordering the required amount of ready-mixed concrete in 3 or 6 cubic yard loads. The delivery lorry will require up to 8ft. clearance between gateposts if it is to be delivered where you want it, otherwise you will need several helpers to barrow it in since it should all be used within one hour of delivery.

Strong boards should be placed and fixed with pegs to mark the drive area and these should be about 3in. above ground level to give you the thickness of concrete you require.

Laying a drive this way is not be recommended unless you can get considerable help at the time the concrete is delivered.

However the method has advantages where a large area has to be covered and where a very solid foundation for drive and garage floor must be laid quickly.

The alternative method is to use pre-cast concrete paving slabs by the solid bed method. A little extra care is needed in

126

Four grades of Marleymix are available, each for a specific purpose. These handy bags are ideal for every type of concreting and mortar job.

preparing the foundations which should be well firmed by the addition of hard core well rammed down. Then a layer of cement mortar of about $\frac{3}{4}$in. should be spread—enough to lay one slab at a time. Any contour required to allow rainwater to run off should be decided upon. A slight fall to the edges is all that is necessary. Each slab should be positioned carefully and tapped gently into position and checked with a straight edge. Leave a gap of $\frac{1}{4}$in. between the paving and fill these with a dryish mortar mix after about 48 hours. If you position the slabs close together this results in tighter joints which can result in cracks during extremes of weather.

When you come to path laying there are three methods you can use, shown opposite: Solid Bed, Mortar Spot and the Dry Method. The mortar spot method is quite satisfactory for normal foot traffic, but once again the foundations should be compacted and levelled. Over this a layer of sand or ashes should be spread and rolled to compact it.

Each slab should now be bedded on one to five evenly placed mortar blobs, depending on the size of the paving. The recommendation is to use one spot or blob (3-4in. across) in the centre of a 12in. × 12in. slab while a 24in. square slab should have five spots—one at each corner and one in the centre.

The slab should then be gently pressed into the mortar and checked with a straight edge. Leave to set for at least 48 hours when the slabs can be pointed up as described above.

The Dry Method is of course the cheapest and is quite suitable for occasionally used paths although unless careful compaction of the subsoil is done there can be occasional settlement requiring attention.

When the foundation is ready, fine soil, sand or ashes should be spread to a depth of at least $\frac{1}{2}$in. and the slabs carefully placed in position and lightly bedded down. Leave narrow joints and fill these with a dryish mortar mix when you are satisfied the path is level.

When necessary, cutting the slabs should be done this way: the paving should be laid on a bed of sand or soft soil—never on a hard surface. Mark the line or place where the cut is required on both sides with a cold chisel. Stand the paving on its edge and nick the edges where the lines are to a depth of $\frac{1}{4}$in. Now lay the paving flat and with hammer and cold chisel score along the lines. Do this on both sides and repeat the process scoring a little deeper each time. Increasing the strength of the hammer

blows will soon result in the paving breaking cleanly along the marked lines.

Marley Landscape Paving for terraces, paths, surrounds, drives, garden and landscape features is available in an attractive range of colours, textures and sizes.

Colourstone, for example, can be purchased in five mellow shades of marigold, sea grey, stone, heather and brick. The surface has the appearance of sawn stone and is safer to walk on than smooth top paving.

It is available in six rectangular sizes the metric equivalents of 9in. x 9in., 12in. x 12in., 18in. x 9in., 18in. x 18in., 24in. x 12in. and 24in. x 24in., but it can be obtained in hexagonal and circular form also.

The hexagonal is based upon a 600mm. module (approx. 24in.) and in half-size pavings used for finishing the edges of rectangular areas. The circular paving, useful for setting in lawns or as stepping stones are 450mm. (approx. 18in.) across.

Marlstone is quite different. This has a textured natural finish

A typical patio laid with Marley Colourstone paving and walling units.

130

as in hand-tooled stone and can be laid in a variety of attractive patterns from its three sizes of 12in. x 12in., 24in. x 12in. and 24in. x 24in.

Did you know you can now get pre-cast Cobblestone? Marley have now produced this in an attractive dark grey colour and it is particularly effective when used to break up a large area of paving or as a centre of a drive where oil marks from parked vehicles will not look so unsightly. Cobblestone is supplied in slabs 600mm. x 600mm. (approx. 24in. x 24in.).

The most recent addition to the paving range—and most appealing—is Colourstone Contour providing an opportunity to plan architectural features. Two alternative sizes, both with their complementary half sizes are made to the latest modular metric dimensions and either may be used individually or together. Made to metric dimensions the sizes are approximately 14in. narrowing to 5in., and 26in. narrowing to 14in. with half sizes, which means that there are six sizes altogether and these are all available in the five Colourstone pastel colours.

The great merit of Contour is that curved paths, circular features—such as round a circular pond, rotary clothes line, bird bath, etc.—can now be laid without unsightly infilling of the gaps if rectangular paving is used.

All Marley Landscape Paving has a nominal thickness of $1\frac{1}{2}$in. (38mm.). In addition the range of concrete products includes Marley Garden Edging and Colourstone Walling. The former is in pieces 3ft. long, 7in. high and 2in. thick (914mm. x 178mm. x 51mm.) with a rounded top edge. This is used as a permanent edging for paths, terraces, patios, flower beds. The latter is based upon Colourstone Paving 18in. x 9in. with a coping of 24in. x 12in.

In addition to walling from paving, Marley produces decorative screen walling blocks in three patterns and two colours, Windsor Grey and Stone, and, of course, pilaster blocks, caps and copings to use with them. The screen walling units in Bermuda, Barbados and Bahama designs are each $11\frac{5}{8}$in. x $11\frac{5}{8}$in. x $3\frac{5}{8}$in. (295 x 295 x 92mm.). The Pilaster blocks are $7\frac{5}{8}$in. x $7\frac{5}{8}$in. x $7\frac{5}{8}$in. (194mm.), the caps $8\frac{1}{8}$in. x $8\frac{1}{8}$in. x $1\frac{1}{2}$in. and the copings can be flat $23\frac{1}{2}$in. x $5\frac{1}{2}$in. x $1\frac{1}{2}$in. or twice-weathered $23\frac{1}{2}$in. x $5\frac{1}{2}$in. x $1\frac{1}{2}$in. to $\frac{3}{4}$in. These walling units are non load-bearing and should be laid on a concrete foundation strip in a trench, the depth of foundation depending upon the height of the wall.

For heights of up to 2ft. the foundation should be 9in. wide

Screen walling blocks are available in three patterns and two colours of Windsor Grey and Stone. Pilaster blocks, caps and copings can be obtained at Marley Buildings showgrounds.

6in. deep and no reinforcement of the pilasters is required. Up to 4ft. foundation should be 1ft. wide by 6in. deep and pilasters should be placed at 8ft. spacings, without reinforcement but filled with fine concrete mix. Four feet to six feet walls need a foundation of 15in. wide × 10in. deep and a $\frac{1}{2}$ in. diameter mild steel rod should be inserted in the pilasters. A horizontal galvanised reinforcement is recommended for the top courses of the walling units. Both of these aids are available from most builders' merchants.

In your garden

(

If you own, or will own, the freehold of your property have you ever stopped to think about its value, even after you have read that building land in the suburbs of the bigger cities is fetching as much as £10,000 for one-quarter-of-an-acre during 1972?

Think this over. If your house stands on a plot of, say, 100ft. by 54ft. you have in fact almost one-eighth of an acre so on the above calculations you have, and belonging only to YOU, land worth in the region of £5,000. Even half this size of 50ft. by 27ft. is worth over £2,000.

If you accept these figures you will appreciate the argument that every square foot surrounding your house is a precious commodity and should be developed as an asset and not left to become an eyesore or a menace to the fabric of your property.

The neglected, weedy front garden, the overgrown jungle at the rear are sufficient evidence of a don't care attitude and they de-value your property, often in a startling way.

Many a house sale has fallen through when a prospective buyer has taken a look around a newly painted house with a neat interior and then found the obvious signs of neglect outside. He is likely to be suspicious that all is not quite what it seems. So everything must be brought up to a better standard and there's no better place to start than the fencing.

Fencing

For years it was the custom to use an all-timber construction for close-boarded fencing, sinking the posts in the wet soil and surrounding them with great clods of concrete to produce a quick result. The practice was a bad one even when the timber had been soaked in creosote, for there's plenty of evidence to be seen in fallen fences and propped up posts that decay had soon set in. When a timber gravel board was placed on the ground this was usually the first place for decay and wet rot to enter.

Three distinct types of walling for boundaries are made by Marley Buildings. The styles are shown here and described in detail. A colour leaflet is freely available.

However if your present fence is in fairly good condition and only the supports need to be replaced and you want to economise on repair costs, reinforced concrete spur posts 4in. x 4in. 3ft. 6in. lengths should be used. Marley Fence Savers are ideal for this purpose and incorporate a brown colouring additive which tones with most treated timber thus providing a most unobtrusive support. The posts are drilled in two pieces for $8\frac{1}{2}$in. x $\frac{3}{8}$in. bolts and cost complete not much more than £1.00.

Having fixed the fence upright by means of an angled batten or prop, remove the earth and any decayed stump and place the Fence Saver 18in. into the soil. Ram the soil well down and drill the fence post to take the bolts. Tighten the nuts and washers and then finish off with a 12in. depth of concrete 1 : 2 : 4 mix. Leave the batten support for 24 hours for the concrete to harden, especially if you are dealing with a closeboard fence in windy weather.

If you have to replace a timber gravel board you can make a much better and longer lasting job by casting a concrete plinth in the same concrete mix. This combination of concrete and timber results in a very firm and long-lasting construction and is the basis for the very popular Marley Defiant Fencing, which makes use of brown-coloured reinforced concrete posts and gravel boards but with close-fitting timber panels made from selected larch or Douglas fir with wavey-edged horizontal slats. Each panel incorporates a weathered capping piece but normally supplied with fencing panels. The panels are treated with a golden brown preservative, and fit into special recesses in the posts and gravel boards. Three heights of fence are 4ft., 5ft. and 6ft. from ground level to top of panels and posts should be inserted into the ground at 18in., 24in. and 30in. respectively.

Standard panel widths are 6ft. 6in. at post centres but 5ft. 6in., 4ft. 8in., 4ft., 3ft. 6in. and 3ft. 2in. bays are available.

If you are looking for a fencing or walling system in a contemporary design idiom there are four other types which may appeal.

The first is called Concord, similar to Defiant, but with posts and 12in. deep bottom panels of Sparlite faced reinforced concrete; Ranch Walling for partial screening in 3ft., 4ft. 6in. and 6ft. heights of concrete panels with one side faced in Sparlite; Vanguard Walling in concrete for complete privacy and enclosure and an exciting new Mini-Walling.

The latter type, subject of a patent, is produced in one

standard height of 18in. (450mm.) above ground level, comprised of 12in. deep (300mm.) panels with two integral posts forming a one piece unit. One side is faced with Sparlite. This easily erected mini-wall is available in two lengths for erection at 6ft. 6¾in. (2m.) and 4ft. 11in. (1.5m.) centres. The posts are inserted into the ground to a depth of 1ft. 5¾in. (0.450m.).

Incidentally all these fences and walling system are for self-assembly, but for jobs of a reasonable size it is possible to get them done by a team of skilled erectors.

When considering the replacement of a fence or wall it should be noted that there may be regulations which must be observed especially in the many new estates based upon the open planning principle.

The common rule of fencing or walling not higher than 3ft. in the front of the house and 7ft. at the rear may apply and there is always the question of which fence or wall belongs to you, especially in terraced and semi-detached properties.

It was also considered that when a close board fence is erected, the best side (without the arris rail) is facing your neighbour's property but this is not supported in law because it inevitably means that if such a fence is erected on the boundary you must 'trespass on your neighbour's land' in order to nail the boards to the arris rail.

However with all the types of fencing described in this chapter there is no question of invading any property other than your own. One of the biggest developments in fencing which has become very popular, not only on account of its low cost, ease of erection and maintenance is Vinyl Fencing, particularly favoured by those who need a clear boundary demarcation and a means of preventing children or tradesmen from wandering across flower beds and lawns.

This fencing is built up stage by stage of three basic components—a white, rigid PVC box section plank 5ft. or 10ft. long, 4in. (101.6mm.) wide and ¾in. (19.1mm.) thick, posts either 3ft. 3in. (991mm.) and 4ft. 6in. (1.371m.) high inserted at least a third of the overall height below the ground.

The posts are formed to take two or three rails but if wooden posts are preferred the rails may be fixed with galvanised bolts as shown. The fixing instructions are quite straightforward.

Posts should be set in ground in concrete. Marleymix 1 : 2 : 4 is ideal for this purpose and a large bag should be sufficient for five or six posts. Once the posts are set in the ground, the rails are slotted in the apertures provided and the locking device ensures that they do not come out again. The top of the post is masked with a capping piece which provides a weatherproof finish. Posts should not normally be at more than 1.524m. (5ft.) centres and should be at least a third of the overall height below the ground.

When erecting a Marley Post and Plank Fence, proceed as follows:

1 Set posts in holes previously dug out and back-fill with concrete.

2 Allow concrete to set.

3 Slide planks into holes in posts. Make sure that the slot in the planks is facing the ground and push the plank into the apertures in the post. This is a tight fit and when the locking slot has found the post wall it will drop down and lock so that the plank is fixed. This system allows for controlled thermal movement in the vinyl plank.

4 If a plank has to be cut so that the locking device is removed, a fresh one can be fabricated by cutting the end of the plank and using a pair of pliers to elevate the nib. (See sketch A & B, page 139).

An adhesive may be used on the post caps if there is any danger of vandals removing them. The clear type of adhesive is suitable for this purpose.

Gates

As this fencing has grown in popularity the need arose for a matching garden gate and this is now available in the shape of the Ashford. Also made of white vinyl, including catches and hinges, the gate can be used in conjunction with the three-plank fencing or on its own as a decorative gate.

It is supplied with hanging and slamming posts, slotted if used with the fencing or unslotted if you want it so and fixing is simple. If used with the vinyl fencing you proceed as follows:
Dig out holes on each side of the gate 30in. apart and set the hanging and slamming posts in position. Hang the gate and check that it will swing freely and lock on the slamming post catch. The slamming post catch is adjustable. When posts are correctly set for position and height above the ground, temporarily hold in place with wooden struts and back-fill holes with concrete. Marleymix is ideal for this purpose.

When concrete is set slot planks into apertures in posts as for the remainder of the Marley Fence. Fig. B.

Marley Vinyl Fencing has set a new standard for permanent maintenance free fencing. It is available in 2 or 3 plank styles, has only 3 components and is simple to erect. A matching latch gate—the Ashford—completes a most attractive fence arrangement.

FIXING INSTRUCTIONS

Post should be set in the ground in concrete. Marleymix 1-2-4 is ideal for this purpose and a large bag should be sufficient for five/six posts. Once the posts are set in the ground, the rails are slotted in the apertures provided and the locking device ensures that they do not come out again. The top of the post is masked with a capping piece which provides a weatherproof finish. Posts should not normally be at more than 1·524m (5') centres and should be at least $\frac{1}{3}$rd of the overall height below the ground. When erecting a Marley Post and Plank Fence, proceed as follows:

1 Set posts in holes previously dug out and back-fill with concrete.

2 Allow concrete to set.

3 Slot planks into holes in posts. The locking nib will spring up inside the post to prevent the plank from being displaced.

4 If a plank has to be cut so that the locking nib is removed, a fresh one can be fabricated by cutting the end of the plank and using a pair of pliers to elevate the nib (See sketch a and b).

Note An adhesive may be used on the post caps if there is any danger of vandals removing them. A clear Bostic type adhesive is suitable for this purpose.

Technical Data
Material Unplasticised Rigid PVC.
Thermal Expansion 0·043 in/ft 100°F.
Flame Spread Self extinguishing, no spread of flame.
Colours White only.
Stock Lengths 1·524m (5') and 3·048m (10')
Planks, Posts 0·991m (3' 3'') and 1·234m (4' 6'') high (end, through, 3-way and 90° angles). (See drawings)

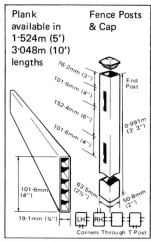

Plank available in 1·524m (5') 3·048m (10') lengths. Fence Posts & Cap

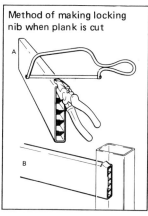

Method of making locking nib when plank is cut

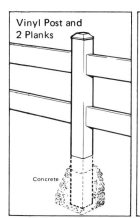

Vinyl Post and 2 Planks

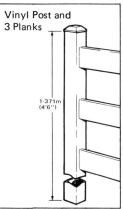

Vinyl Post and 3 Planks

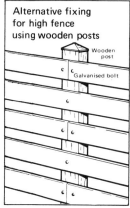

Alternative fixing for high fence using wooden posts

When fixing the gate in an existing hedge proceed as above except that planks are not slotted into the posts.

Porches and entrance halls

Many smaller houses, particularly the suburban semi-detached, are so constructed that the front door opens directly on to a tiny hall offering little or no accommodation for essential outdoor wear. And where there are small children, lack of storage for the pram and muddy boots often leads to argument and distress. Problems such as these can be solved by adding a porch to either the front or back of the dwelling and this, in every case, cuts down draughts, provides a handy store for daytime deliveries and a temporary shelter for visitors. As an addition to your property it must enhance its value.

The addition of a porch is a structural alteration to your house so local authority is necessary and an application form should be obtained. Permission is not usually withheld if the council is convinced that the porch you propose to erect is one which satisfies the requirements of the building regulations and would not be out of keeping with adjacent property.

Marley Buildings make a comprehensive range of Weather Porches specifically designed for erection by the do-it-yourself enthusiast based upon a framework of Western Red Cedar which may be left in its natural state or painted to match your house. Many styles are possible in three basic designs. You can have glass to ground level, or cill height wall panels in one of two finishes, 'Whitespar' or 'Marleybrick'.

There is a draught lobby without a door where the open end can face either way, a porch for houses where the front or back door is sited in an 'L' shaped recess and a three sided fully enclosed porch giving maximum protection to house doors that are flush with the external wall.

There is a choice of two heights of 7ft. and 8ft. and as many as 19 standard layouts shown on a fully comprehensive leaflet which you should get so that you can work out exactly what you want.

As the frames and wall panels are in modules, planning is fairly easy. Frames are 6ft. 8in. high by 1ft., 2ft., 3ft. and 4ft. side. Fanlights are 1ft. x 1ft., 2ft. 3ft. and 4ft. Doors are 6ft. 8in. x 3ft. Frames are fitted with cills incorporating a weather drip. Doors have a weather bar in the frame and are supplied hung complete with mortice lock, and quality door furniture with satin silver finish.

A Weatherporch not only contributes to the value of your property but provides useful additional storage for outdoor gear. Marley Weather Porches are available in two heights of 7ft. and 8ft. and there are 19 standard layouts from which you can choose one to suit your needs.

Wall panels are of 3in. thick reinforced concrete with either Whitespar exposed aggregate or the brick finish. Cill height panels are 2ft. 4in. high, full height panels 6ft. 8in. or 7ft. 8in. The latter combined with an internal chipboard lining give a half-hour fire resistance required in the Building Regulations. Windows above wall panels are 4ft. $4\frac{1}{2}$in. high. The roof is chipboard covered by two layers of felt the top layer being asbestos based and surfaced with stone chippings. Five inch deep cedar fascias with aluminium trim conceal the roof and vinyl gutter which drains into a 2in. downpipe. Glass is 24 and 32oz. and is supplied with glazing beads and putty.

Garage doors

With all the improvements you make to the exterior of your house you may consider that you need to replace worn out garage doors and here again Marley have five distinct types of Autodors to offer at very competitive prices. They are, Timber, Galvasteel, Teakcote, Aluminium and Cedar, all of course, are of the up-and-over type.

These garage doors work on robust coil springs and canti-levered steel side arms and provide maximum clearance immediately inside the door opening. The nylon wheels glide smoothly in the horizontal tracks to ensure that the door is fully housed inside the garage when open. Many local authorities insist upon this form when the front elevation of a garage borders on a public footpath or road.

Door opening sizes are 7ft. x 6ft. 6in. or 7ft. 6in. x 6ft. 6in. with the aluminium type in two larger sizes of 11ft. $0\frac{1}{2}$in. x 6ft. 6in. and 15ft. $0\frac{1}{2}$in. x 6ft. 6in. A new gal-vanised Autodor measuring 14ft x 7ft. has been introduced to cater for the increased number of double garages being built.

Outhouses

There are two other exterior improvement features which should be mentioned—Dustbin Houses and Fuel Bunkers.

The Dustbin House is simply panels of reinforced concrete with the exposed surfaces of top, side and rear units faced with Sparlite stone aggregate finish and a concrete base panel. A single unit has internal measurements of 3ft. high, 1ft. 11in. wide and 1ft. $10\frac{5}{8}$in. deep. The double unit has an internal width of 3ft. 10in. The advantages of having this sturdy storage for your dustbins are obvious.

Marley Fuel Bunkers are available in 6cwt. (13.2cu. ft.),

For garages, sun lounges, workshops and sheds the Marley 3in gutter and two inch pipe fittings are most suitable. The range of fittings and fixing methods is illustrated here.

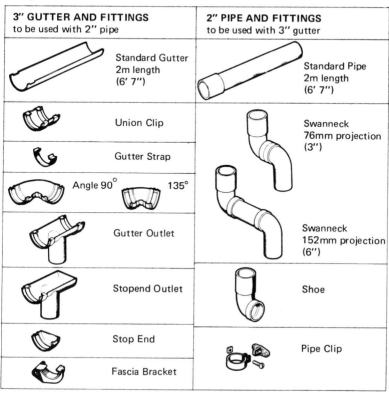

3" GUTTER AND FITTINGS to be used with 2" pipe	2" PIPE AND FITTINGS to be used with 3" gutter
Standard Gutter 2m length (6' 7")	Standard Pipe 2m length (6' 7")
Union Clip	Swanneck 76mm projection (3")
Gutter Strap	
Angle 90° 135°	
Gutter Outlet	Swanneck 152mm projection (6")
Stopend Outlet	Shoe
Stop End	Pipe Clip
Fascia Bracket	

Marley's rainwater goods made from Vinyl are lightweight, easy to handle and will not corrode nor need painting.

143

HOW TO FIX
Patent gutter joint
Incorporating Neoprene gaskets
No sealing compounds required

gutter also available in
4in (100mm)
ask for details

D This installation can be assembled at ground level, bracket positions marked on fascia and spacings MUST NOT EXCEED 1m (3' 3") CENTRES. Gutters then lifted and turned into position as in B.

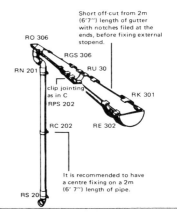

Short off-cut from 2m (6' 7") length of gutter with notches filed at the ends, before fixing external stopend.

RO 306
RN 201
RGS 306
RU 30
clip jointing as in C
RPS 202
RK 301
RC 202
RE 302
RS 20

It is recommended to have a centre fixing on a 2m (6' 7") length of pipe.

A Clip gutter into the socket under the retaining nibs to complete joint. Whenever a 2m (6' 7") length of gutter is cut, notches must be filed on the gutter ends to the same dimensions as those supplied with the full 2m (6' 7") lengths.

B Vinyl gutter bracket (RK 301) screwed into position on fascia. Method of introducing 3in (75mm) gutter in brackets in order to ensure that the gutter is held securely.

E If it is not possible to fix brackets to the framework on a greenhouse then a 2in (50·8mm) x ½in (12·7mm) fascia should be fixed across the glazing bars.

C Note position of fascia brackets near to each side of the union clip (RU 30). BRACKET SPACINGS MUST NOT EXCEED 1m (3' 3") CENTRES. Join gutter lengths together by using a union clip (RU 30) as shown.

Note:
Angles RA 304, RA 306 and the stopend RE 302 are jointed to gutter by fitting the gutter strap RD 30 around the socket, then the gutter is clipped into position as in A.

144

9cwt. (20.6cu. ft.) and 12cwt. (26.8cu. ft.) single models and also in twin sizes. They are made of precast concrete in either terra cotta or grey colours and have a large galvanised steel lid. Concrete non-spill hoppers and base units are available as optional extras.

Patios

As every square foot of land you have is precious it should be used to the best advantage. Even the 'pocket-handkerchief' sized plot attached to town houses can provide very pleasant areas for children to play in and parents to relax.

In the smaller areas paved patios are more suitable than lawns which can rarely be maintained where there is much traffic in wet weather. But there is no need for these areas to be drab. There is a great variety of containers available today in which shapely conifers or bedding plants can be grown. Oak tubs are quite cheap and if the interiors are given two applications of a good preservative and the exteriors regularly treated with varnish or linseed oil they will last a lifetime. The preservative to use is green Cuprinol which is a recommended wood preservative which does not affect growing plants.

All planting containers should have adequate drainage and it is a good plan to see that if they are of wood they should be so placed on the paving that air can circulate underneath them. When choosing evergreen conifers for planting in containers or in gaps in the paving it is essential to choose the slower-growing dwarf varieties. Your local garden centre will advise you on this. Try to get a mixed collection as there are many to choose from, of different shape and different colours which remain almost constant through the growing season.

If the woman of the house takes a pride in her cooking it is possible to have a small herb garden if you can find a sunny corner. Parsley, for instance, grows well as a path edging, and a few small plants of thyme look most attractive when set into small gaps in the paving.

Really colourful patios can be achieved if you are prepared to go to a little trouble and you can do it very much on the cheap if you grow your own plants.

While many people with very small gardens are quite successful in raising sufficient plants by sowing the seeds in small boxes placed upon a sunny windowsill it is a much simpler (and more interesting) if you make yourself a simple garden frame. The simplest construction of all is to secure a sheet of

A POOL MADE IN A WEEKEND

A hole is dug, the excavated soil distributed round the garden, or dumped, and a plastic liner is placed upon a soft bed of sand, peat or even several layers of newspapers. This is to prevent sharp stones piercing the liner when the pond is filled.

Calculate the size of liner this way. Length of pool plus twice its depth by width of pool plus twice its depth. So that a pool 9ft. long by 6ft. wide and 2ft.6in. deep requires a liner size of 14ft. by 11ft. This will allow for a shelf 9in. deep by 9in. wide round part of the pool to accommodate marginal plants, (which do not require deep water), in polythene crates.

The picture sequence shows an enlarged ovate shaped pool being levelled, the liner supported by bricks while the pond is being filled so that it stretches slightly to take up the shape of the excavation and avoid unnecessary pleats. The final picture was taken one year after construction. All plants and lilies are well established and there is an ever-increasing family of fish.

1

2

3

4

5

Marleyglaze to a framework of 1½ × 1in. timber and this will give you a cover of almost 15sq. ft. area.

The sides can be made from 12in. square slabs of paving sunk 3in. into the soil on 2in. thick blobs of cement mortar. When this has set a little of the soil in the frame can be lifted out to give space for a layer of sand upon which pans of seeds or seed boxes can be planted.

As the Marleyglaze cover is very light it is easily lifted off to tend the growing plants but in exposed positions where the cover is likely to be lifted off in a high wind it should be secured by wiring it to wooden pegs driven into the soil at each corner of the frame.

This simple kind of frame can be used to overwinter plants such as geraniums and fuchsias if the insides of the frame are covered with 1in. thick pieces of Marleycel expanded poly-styrene and the top covered with sacking and polythene in times of severe frost. With this slightly sunken flat-topped type of frame it is advisable to have one end very slightly higher than the other so that rainwater will drain off from the cover.

A Marleyglaze panel of this type has many other uses. If you make several of them and hinge them together they make a most attractive screen and if adequately secured make a most effective windbreak.

A single panel makes a most useful cover for a children's sand-pit which can be constructed in a way similar to that of the garden frame. If you do make a sand pit fill it with washed river sand. If you use the ordinary builder's sand it can stain the children's clothing.

Pools and ponds

A garden pool adds tremendous interest to any garden but is certainly not advisable where there are young toddlers. But they will delight in splashing about in a couple of inches of water. This can be provided very simply by a portable plastic container or by spreading a sheet of thick blue polythene over the sand-pit or in a suitable surround of sunken paving slabs.

But for the keen gardener who wants to build a garden pond there is no limit to what he can do. The simplest way is merely to dig a hole and insert either a pre-formed glassfibre pool or to line the hole with sand and insert a butyl rubber or plastic liner to a carefully measured size and let the water run in. The surround can be built from any of the varieties of Landscape Paving. More detailed information on garden ponds is out of place here but there are many specialist water garden companies whose catalogues explain in great detail what can be done and where the aquatic plants and fish can be obtained.

The greenhouse

From every point of view a greenhouse is an essential requirement for anyone really interested in making the most of his garden whether the latter is a small enclosed area at the rear of a town house or a quarter-of-an-acre space in a woodland setting. For apart from greatly extending his knowledge of garden plants and their growth from seed to bedding-out time it gives him undercover time when conditions outside may be very unpleasant. With a properly designed and equipped greenhouse you can grow plants very much more cheaply than you can buy them and you can grow the special choice varieties you want rather than those often mediocre standard varieties of plants bought elsewhere.

But of all the advantages none is greater than the opportunity provided by a greenhouse of a fascinating hobby for all the year round. Owners of greenhouses will readily tell you that choice is all-important and a construction that offers maximum light, controlled ventilation and minimum maintenance is the one to buy. And you certainly want one that is strong and which will not sag at the ridge or give way to stresses on the glass in gale-force winds. Add to this; ease of erection or dismantling, and your choice will lie in a modern aluminium and stainless steel construction which will not rot, warp or need any maintenance.

The new range of Marley greenhouses satisfies all these requirements, for each basic design, efficient as a single unit can be extended as you desire.

The Chelsea greenhouse range has a width of 6ft. $2\frac{3}{4}$in., its height on concrete plinth units is 6ft. 10in. to ridge and 5ft. 2in. to eaves and gives more than usual working height. Each has a sliding door. The lengths are 5ft. 1in., 7ft. 6in., 9ft. $11\frac{1}{8}$in., and 12ft. $4\frac{1}{4}$in., with one roof ventilator in the two smaller models and two in the larger ones.

The Sunningdale range has widths of 7ft. $3\frac{1}{4}$in., giving a ridge height of 6ft. 11in., with three lengths of 7ft. 6in., 9ft. $11\frac{1}{8}$in. and 12ft. $4\frac{1}{4}$in.

Erection of the greenhouse is simple enough—there's no drilling or cutting, merely a bolting together job with clipping in the pre-cut glass For very tall gardeners who want increased

148

working height Marley provide concrete plinth units which are much easier to lay than bricks.

Merit points in these greenhouses are the clear door opening of 2ft. 4in., the centre rail of mahogany and the design of the bottom door runner which prevents the accumulation of dirt and grit usually evident in these channels; full length glass to avoid discoloured overlaps; hinged ventilators with locking stay, special channels to collect condensation water from the roof and, in the wider models an integral aluminium gutter.

A full range of optional extras, ventilators, roll-shades, automatic ventilator opener, staging, shelf brackets and heating equipment is also available.

A brilliant new range of high class Aluminium Greenhouses is now available from Marley Buildings. This is model B1, the Sunningdale 7ft3¼in long, 7ft6in wide. Cost about £60.50.

⑬
Some problems discussed

Roof repairs
While the competent DIY man, who has access to the right equipment and has had some experience of working at heights, can adequately deal with repairs and renewal of roofing it is not a job for the uninitiated.

Marley Ltd., have just announced a re-roofing improvement plan on a tax-relief loan plan advance scheme.

A comprehensive leaflet describes some of the roof faults you may have; inadequate felt protection, cracked and slipping tiles, decayed or missing tiles, sagging timbers, lamination or flaking of clay tiles, etc.

Under the scheme, specialists of the company will remove all existing slates or tiles, check and replace timbers where necessary, fit new underlay, fit new Marley tiles to your choice of colour and shape, renew gutters and leadwork and chimney flashings as necessary.

The cost is surprisingly modest. Easy terms are available with tax relief and are covered by free life insurance.

The tiles are guaranteed for 50 years and the workmanship for 10 years.

If this interests you, contact Marley at Sevenoaks for further details and estimates.

Rising damp
Rising damp is a phrase often used by persons who are worried by the appearance of dampness in the lower floors of their property. But in many cases it is not dampness at all but the result of condensation.

In its true form it is dampness which creeps by capillary action up into porous materials because of pressure from water in adjacent areas. Water always tends to find its own level and for this reason a dampcourse, or dpc as it is commonly known, should always be present in the foundations of your house. It should extend across the whole of the platform or raft on which

150

your property stands and, while most new houses have their concrete bases sealed from contact with the soil by a layer of polythene sheeting and the brickwork separated from soil contact by a thin layer of some waterproof strip, there are many houses which have neither. To insert a dpc in these houses is a costly job.

If you suspect you have rising damp on any of the solid floors of your house, which means that tiles have lifted, or suspended floors seem damp, there is one simple test you can apply: wipe over with a dry cloth any suspected area and place over it a $\frac{1}{2}$ in. thick ring about 3in. diameter of a substance such as Plasticine or mastic and immediately press on this ring a piece of dry glass so that you seal the enclosed area. Leave it for 24 hours before you examine it. If the underside of the glass shows the presence of any moisture this will tell you that damp has entered from below.

If the floor is a solid one every effort should be made to dry it out and when this has been done the whole floor should be given two coats of a special preparation based upon a mixture of epoxy resin and pitch. Your retailer will advise you on this. If the trouble is with suspended floors a floorboard should be lifted and the cause located.

In most cases rising damp is associated with external walls and the likely cause is that the original dpc has been covered up by earth piled over it. This should be cleared away and the damp area allowed to dry out.

When damp patches are evident on the interior of lower walls the cause may be that in building the house a careless bricklayer has dropped lumps of mortar which have landed on the metal ties joining the cavity walls and this mortar is transferring dampness from the outer wall. The remedy is to knock out a brick and investigate.

Damp patches on interior walls are often merely the result of condensation and are often found on North facing walls in centrally heated houses where humidity is high. If nothing can be done to increase the number of air changes in the room to reduce humidity you should try the effect of applying an expanded polystyrene wall veneer to the area and repaper over it. This will keep the wall warmer and the condensation will not be obvious.

Plumbing problems

In older houses where the water supplies are still fed from lead pipes, connecting new baths, basins, loos, etc., can present problems which are outside your scope unless you have the ability to 'wipe a joint', to connect lengths of copper tubing to the old supply pipes. But once you have made a sound connection the rest is fairly easy with the compression fittings you can buy today. To make a wiped soldered joint you need a blowtorch and a stick of plumbers' solder, some plumbers' black and tallow, a tapered wooden turnpin to tap into the lead pipe to open it up to receive the new extension of copper pipe or connecting joint, a file or rasp and a 'moleskin' wiping cloth.

The lead pipe is opened up to receive the chamfered end of the copper pipe so that when inserted it is a close fit, but leaving a slight gap so that molten solder can be run into it.

Plumbers' black should be applied equally to each pipe to restrict the length of the join (solder will not adhere to this material) which should be about $2\frac{1}{2}$ to 3in. on $\frac{1}{2}$in. or $\frac{3}{4}$in. diameter pipes. The surfaces of the two pipes where the solder is to be applied should be filed or rasped to clean bright metal and immediately covered with tallow to prevent oxidation and to act as a flux. The joint should now be heated with the blowtorch and rubbed with the solder stick to tin the surface. This is the critical stage for as soon as the solder begins to melt it should be smoothed round the joint with the moleskin held in the palm of the hand.

Keeping the blowtorch going, more solder can be applied and wiped round to give the traditional bellied joint.

A similar method can be used to insert a length of copper pipe into an existing vertical length of lead with this difference. As the lead pipe must be opened and the internal surfaces cleaned, a plug of cotton wool attached to a string should be pushed into the lead pipe. The pipe can then be reamed out to take the chamfered end of the copper one. The plug is then pulled out gently with the scraps of lead you have removed, the end of the copper pipe should be tinned as in normal soldering and pushed into the lead. The gap remaining is then filled with molten solder to give a strong watertight joint.

If you can master these techniques the fitting of baths, etc., and the replacement of old taps with the new types which are most attractive in their styles and colours will come easily to you. However if your water service system is modern and made up of copper tubing you have none of the problems of the old type for the range of compression fittings, elbows, tee pieces, makes the job really simple.

The right adhesive

Even in this age of advanced technology there is no one universal glue which will stick anything to anything or everything to everything. In fact far from looking for one type to satisfy every need science has produced a whole range of adhesives required to cope with the new materials constantly coming onto the market.

It is important therefore to keep to the adhesive recommended for use with the material you propose to use for only in this way can success be achieved.

From their new Adhesives Division Marley have produced this range of products and doubtless there will be more to come.

Vinyl Flooring Adhesives. These are numbered 118, 138 and 148, used for fixing various types of vinyl flooring, jute felt-backed floorings and non-woven nylon carpets.

No. 118, available in 1 pint (568ml.), $\frac{1}{4}$gal. (1.14 litres), $\frac{1}{2}$gal. (2.27 litres), 1gal. (4.54 litres) and 5gal. (22.73 litres). The average coverage of 118 is 20sq. yds. (16.72m.^{2}) per gallon (4.54 litres).

No. 138, especially designed for fixing most backed and unbacked vinyl floorings over concrete screeds containing underfloor heating is available in 1gal. and 5gal. cans.

No. 148 is the high strength, white adhesive for use with Vinylaire and other asbestos-backed floorings and has similar coverage to No. 118.

These three adhesives should be stirred thoroughly before use and spread with a notched spreader. The flooring should be laid while the adhesive is wet, with one exception and that is when the flooring is laid on a non-porous surface. In this case the adhesive should be allowed to become touch-dry.

No. 148 is available in 10fl. oz., $\frac{1}{2}$gal., 1gal. and 5gal. containers.

No. 124 adhesive is for use with expanded polystyrene ceiling tiles and coving and a pint will be needed to fix approx. 30 12in. x 12in. tiles or 200ft. run of coving. It is available in 10fl. oz . and 20fl. oz. tubes, 1 pint, $\frac{1}{4}$gal., $\frac{1}{2}$gal. and 1gal. cans.

Adhesive No. 130 is for use with expanded polystyrene wall veneer and 1gal. is sufficient for 8 rolls of veneer or 35sq. yds. When applying wall veneer the adhesive should be brushed onto the wall. Available in $\frac{1}{4}$gal., $\frac{1}{2}$gal. and 1gal. cans.

For ceramic wall tiles No. 133 adhesive is specified giving an average coverage of 8sq. yds. per gallon. It is packed in 8fl. oz. tubes, $\frac{1}{2}$gal. and 1gal. cans.

In addition there is an All-bond pva adhesive for timber joints and as an additive to concrete bonding work.

All-bond is a plasticised pva adhesive and can be used on timber, plywood, hardboard, aluminium to wood, carpets to concrete, asbestos, plasterboard, cloth and backed vinyl wall coverings. It is not recommended for PVC, polythene or for vessels to contain hot liquids. Packed in 4fl. oz. tubes, 1gal., 5gal. and 45gal.

Floor care

Another important aspect to consider in the appearance of a well-kept home is the floorings, whether they be of traditional timber, carpet or in the modern counterpart of vinyl sheet and tiles. It is worth noting these simple rules.

Radiators should not radiate directly on to the floor. There should be ample space between an open fire and resilient floor. Never put hot objects on the floor. Do not use paraffin or spirit of any kind as a cleaner, or solid wax pastes or liquid waxes which may contain spirit solvents.

Always support heavy furniture on large flat-based furniture shoes. Studs or domed gliders should never rest directly on the floor as they can cause indentations. Movable furniture should have wide-based types of castors and, if these are rubber faced, should move freely on their axles otherwise they will leave black marks.

Fit hard plastic shoes to all chair legs to distribute the weight over a large area.

Dirt and food spillage should be removed by damp mopping and a solution of a special cleaner.

Marley have four well established products which will keep your floors in superb condition.

Floor Cleaner is a concentrated cleaner and floor polish remover. It should be used in the ratio of 1 part cleaner to 50 parts hot water—about $\frac{1}{2}$cupful to one gallon of water. The cleaner is packed in $\frac{1}{2}$ pint, 1 pint and 1gal. containers.

Clearseal Floor Polish is a dri-bright plastic resin emulsion floor polish which dries to a shine without polishing and gives a finish that is scuff resistant. It discourages rubber heel markings and stops the penetration of dirt. Damp mopping restores the original shine. Packed in $\frac{1}{2}$ litre, 1gal. and 5gal. sizes.

Floor Gloss is a dri-bright metallised emulsion floor polish. It gives a superior gloss and wear resistance and may be cleaned using most household detergents without loss of shine. Packed in 1 pint, 1gal. and 5gal. sizes.

Finally there is Superwax Floor Polish—a semi-buffable emulsion. It dries to a bright shine and can be polished to a high gloss. It gives good resistance to foot marks. Packed in 1 pint, 1gal. and 5gal. containers.

All of these products have been specifically prepared for the wide range of Marley floorings but are also useful for most types of floors including sealed wood block, most cork floors, rubber and asphalt.

Cork tile floorings

As cork is a natural material, not man-made, many people appreciate that it makes an ideal flooring and wall material because of its warmth, durability and insulation against noise and cold. Cork tiles are made from the bark of the evergreen cork oak tree from which the bark is stripped every 10-15 years. The longer it is left the denser it becomes and it is from the denser material that floor tiles are made.

One particulr type, readily available from retail outlets is called Siesta and can be obtained in 12in. squares of $\frac{1}{8}$, $\frac{3}{16}$, $\frac{1}{4}$ and $\frac{5}{16}$in. thicknesses.

They are pre-finished with a hard wax to give a long lasting surface and can be fixed to every type of subfloor providing certain requirements are satisfied. Full instructions are given in a leaflet available from your retailer.

Fitting a new door

When a door, particularly a front one, has passed the stage when repairs to stiles and rails no longer have any effect it must be replaced. You may think this is a costly and difficult job. But it is not so. Your retailer can supply one from quite a large range he has in stock and you should certainly choose one to give your entrance a bit of a face lift.

Examine your present door and frame and measure each very carefully. Check that the frame is perfectly square and that the cill is not worn too badly.

If the frame has twisted—and it may show signs of rot—you will need to replace both. You can get a matching set, but the door will need some preparation to make a good fit.

Door and and frame may be of softwood or hardwood, the latter being considerably more expensive. You will also need new hinges and door furniture (lock or locks, letter plate, etc.).

The hinges must be capable of carrying the weight of the door and your supplier will advise you what to get. You want three brass hinges of at least 4in. particularly if your door is of softwood and likely to warp.

If the frame is square and you need only a new door measure the opening carefully. It will probably be of a standard size about 6ft. 8in. high by 32in. wide. The door size would then be 6ft. 6in. or so by $31\frac{3}{4}$in. to give a close fit against the jambs.

The standard fitting procedure is to place the door against the jamb on the hinge side and mark the door. Any surplus wood more than $\frac{1}{4}$ to $\frac{1}{2}$in. will have to be sawn off, but if you have chosen the size carefully there should not be much. This isn't a particularly easy job without the right equipment of a bench or saw horse but it is essential you keep the saw at right angles or your door top will not be square. Finish off with a plane or power sander.

With the door length settled you must now tackle the width. Place the door on the hinge side jamb and mark again with the pencil. If you have held the door correctly this line should be equidistant from the edge of the door all the way down. If not check again. Once again the surplus should be removed carefully with a plane and the door constantly checked to get a good fit with a thin packing of $\frac{1}{8}$in. inserted at the bottom of the door to make it easy to open.

If the hinges on the frame are sound they can be used again but it is better to replace them. Fit the new hinges into the old positions making sure that they bed in nicely and are not proud of the surface.

Offer up the door with the packing or wedges in place and mark the exact position of the hinges on the door. Lay the hinges on the door and cut the recesses with a chisel.

Now position the door once again on its wedges or packing and fix each hinge with one screw. Test the opening and if satisfactory insert the remaining screws.

A hardwood weather bar should be fitted to all exterior doors.

Index

Metric-Imperial conversion tables

METRIC EQUIVALENTS

Some simple conversion tables. Use the centre
column in bold type and read either side.
Example 10mm = 0.39 inches
        10in   = 254 mm

LENGTH millimetres	mm or inches	inches	WEIGHT kilogrammes	kg or pounds	pounds
25.4	1	0.04	0.45	1	2.21
50.8	2	0.08	0.91	2	4.41
76.2	3	0.12	1.36	3	6.61
101.6	4	0.16	1.81	4	8.82
127.0	5	0.20	2.27	5	11.02
152.4	6	0.24	2.72	6	13.23
177.8	7	0.28	3.18	7	15.43
203.2	8	0.32	3.63	8	17.64
288.6	9	0.35	4.08	9	19.84
254.0	10	0.39	4.54	10	22.05
508.0	20	0.79	9.07	20	44.09
762.0	30	1.18	13.61	30	66.14
1016	40	1.58	18.14	40	88.19
1270	50	1.97	22.68	50	110.2
1524	60	2.36	27.22	60	132.3
1778	70	2.76	31.75	70	154.3
2032	80	3.15	36.29	80	176.4
2286	90	3.54	40.82	90	198.4
2540	100	3.94	45.36	100	220.5

kilometres	km or miles	miles	VOLUME litres	litres or gallons	gallons
1.61	1	0.62	4.55	1	0.22
3.22	2	1.24	9.09	2	0.44
4.83	3	1.86	13.64	3	0.66
6.44	4	2.49	18.18	4	0.88
8.05	5	3.11	22.73	5	1.10
9.66	6	3.73	27.28	6	1.32
11.27	7	4.35	31.82	7	1.54
12.88	8	4.97	36.37	8	1.76
14.48	9	5.59	40.91	9	1.98
16.09	10	6.21	45.46	10	2.20
32.19	20	12.43	90.92	20	4.40
48.28	30	18.64	136.4	30	6.60
64.37	40	24.86	181.8	40	8.80
80.47	50	31.07	227.3	50	11.00
96.56	60	37.28	272.8	60	13.20
112.7	70	43.50	318.2	70	15.40
128.7	80	49.71	363.7	80	17.60
144.8	90	55.92	409.1	90	19.80
160.9	100	62.14	454.6	100	22.00

METRIC MEASURES AND BRITISH EQUIVALENTS

Length
1 millimetre (mm)		= 0·0394 in
1 metre (m)	= 1000 mm	= 1·0936 yds
1 kilometre (km)	= 1000 m	= 0·6214 mile

Surface or Area
1 sq cm (cm^2)	= 100 mm^2	= 0·1550 sq in
1 sq metre (m^2)	= 10,000 cm^2	= 1·1960 sq yds
1 are (a)	= 100 m^2	= 119·60 sq yds
1 hectare (ha)	= 100 ares	= 2·4711 acres
1 sq km (km^2)	= 100 hectares	= 0·3861 sq mile

Capacity
1 cu cm (cm^3)		= 0·0610 cu in
1 cu decimetre (dm^3)	= 1000 cm^3	= 0·0351 cu ft
1 cu metre (m^3)	= 1000 dm^3	= 1·3080 cu yds
1 litre (l)	= 1 dm^3	= 0·2200 gallon
1 hectolitre (hl)	= 100 litres	= 2·7497 bushels

Weight
1 milligramme (mg)		= 0·0154 grain
1 gramme (g)	= 1000 mg	= 0·0353 oz
1 kilogramme (kg)	= 1000 g	= 2·2046 lb
1 tonne (t)	= 1000 kg	= 0·9842 ton

BRITISH MEASURES AND METRIC EQUIVALENTS

Length
1 inch		= 25·4 mm
1 foot	= 12 inches	= 0·3048 m
1 yard	= 3 feet	= 0·9144 m
1 rod	= 5·5 yards	= 5·0292 m
1 chain	= 22 yards	= 20·117 m
1 furlong	= 220 yards	= 201·17 m
1 mile	= 1760 yards	= 1·6093 km
1 nautical mile	= 6080 feet	= 1·8532 km

Surface or Area
1 sq inch		= 6·4516 cm^2
1 sq foot	= 144 sq inches	= 0·0929 m^2
1 sq yard	= 9 sq feet	= 0·8361 m^2
1 acre	= 4840 sq yards	= 4046·86 m^2
1 sq mile	= 640 acres	= 259·0 hectares

Capacity
1 cu inch		= 16·387 cm^3
1 cu foot	= 1728 cu ins	= 0.0283 m^3
1 cu yard	= 27 cu feet	= 0.7646 m^3
1 pint	= 4 gills	= 0.5683 litres
1 quart	= 2 pints	= 1.1365 litres
1 gallon	= 8 pints	= 4.5461 litres
1 bushel	= 8 gallons	= 36.369 litres

Weight
Avoirdupois
1 ounce	= 437.5 grains	= 28.350 gm
1 pound	= 16 ounces	= 0.4536 kg
1 stone	= 14 pounds	= 6.3503 kg
1 hundredweight	= 112 pounds	= 50.802 kg
1 ton	= 20 cwt	= 1.0161 tonnes